Adventure Sports

WHITE WATER
KAYAKING

Adventure Sports

WHITE WATER
KAYAKING

RAY ROWE

Stackpole Books

Cameron and Kelker Streets • P.O. Box 1831 • Harrisburg, PA 17105

A STACKPOLE BOOK

First published in Great Britain by Salamander Books Limited, London 1988 © Salamander Books Ltd

ISBN 0-8117-2284-8

Published by Stackpole Books
Cameron and Kelker Streets
PO Box 1831
Harrisburg, PA 17105
1-800-READ-NOW

Edited and designed by: Curtis Garratt Ltd.
Colour reproductions: Melbourne Graphics Ltd.
Filmset: SX Composing Ltd.
Printed in Belgium by Proost International Book Production, Turnhout.

The author
Ray Rowe was a member of the Irish international kayak racing team for six years and competed throughout Europe. He then became interested in sea kayaking, making a crossing of the Irish Sea. Subsequently, he circumnavigated Ninivak Island in the Bering Sea. He was Head of Canoeing at Plas y Brenin, the National Centre for Mountain Activities, for eight years, where he trained paddlers and coaches in sea, surf, and white-water kayaking. Ray Rowe is now employed by the British Canoe Union. He lectures extensively and runs courses on safety and rescue in white water. He is a regular contributor to *Canoeist* magazine, is the Features Editor for the BCU magazine, *Canoe Focus*, and has compiled the new BCU Handbook.

The illustrator
Ron Brown was originally trained as an engineering prototype fitter. He qualified in technical graphics in 1975 after training at Barking Regional College and the London College of Printing while he was also employed as a full-time technical illustrator. He is currently working as a craft lecturer with unemployed teenagers in further education with the London Borough of Haringey. His interest in canoeing began when he ran basic courses for Edmonton Senior Scouts and Guides, and in recent years he has indulged in canoe surfing and white-water kayaking as a member of the Edmonton Canoe Club and the Sobell Group.

FOREWORD
Whichever aspect of canoeing you take part in, there are certain fundamentals which, if they are observed, will increase your enjoyment of the sport. They are: high-quality instruction; respect for the river; and finally an ability to relax and develop a natural feel for the water. This book will provide paddlers of all levels with a valuable insight into the state of the art of canoeing skills and instruction, and you can do no better than to learn from the knowledge and experience of one of canoeing's true experts.

Ray Rowe is respected throughout the world as a paddler, river leader, and instructor, and few people can speak with the same passion and authority about the sport. My impressions of Ray have been that he embodies all that is the real spirit of canoeing – challenge, excitement, and a sense of adventure – with an infectious enthusiasm. But, if the rivers are up as you read this, go for a paddle and save the book for later. I'm sure Ray would do the same!

Richard Fox MBE
Individual World Slalom Champion 1981, 1983, 1985
World Team Champion 1979, 1981, 1983, 1987

Contents

INTRODUCTION

'We dropped steeply down through the forest looking like a couple of hermit crabs who had just stepped out of their shells to carry them to the water. There was silence now, in contrast to the ceaseless, nervous chatter that rattled around the car interior as we drove out to the river. We emerged from the forest on to the water's edge where the air was filled by the noise of cascading white water. Downstream for about 300 metres (1000 feet) the banks closed in and channelled the water into a steep-sided gorge as if a giant had decided to compress the river between upright hands.

I fumbled with the spray deck, dry mouthed and clumsy handed, until it snapped itself on, ready for action. Andy sent me a brief nod which we both knew meant "Good luck. See you at the other end." Once I was out in the current, the kayak took on the energy of the river. It roared down the ramp that funnelled the water into the gorge with an acceleration which I have often experienced but never got used to. It hurtled through the crashing waves and gaping holes of the rapid while I hung on at the limit of control like a man on a runaway horse. The parts of the rapid which I had so painstakingly memorized sprang into view and then flashed out of sight, lost somewhere in my hypersonic run through the gorge.

In the wide pool at the gorge exit, my journey came to an abrupt end. For a few seconds, my mind continued at meteoric speed and then it sank into a glorious lull. I looked back to see Andy catapulting off the last big wave. His screech of delight filled the whole valley and spilled on to the surrounding mountainsides.'

This memory of a spring day in the mountains of North Wales is one of the delights of white-water paddling from my own experiences. The thrill and excitement of kayaking in a rapid reach so deeply that even the memories can set your pulse racing and the adrenalin surging. Each experience is unique because every river has its own special atmosphere, a personality that cannot be reproduced. Even runs down a familiar river reveal new moods and characteristics which remind you that a river is not an inanimate stretch of water but rather a living, changing entity.

The people who paddle white water have one important thing in common – a desire to challenge themselves. They cannot accept a challenge which is enclosed within the artificial rules and regulations of formalized competition but prefer to tackle the forces of the river on the natural playing fields of the rapids. The rules of the game are self-imposed by the limited supplies of energy which the paddler has at his or her disposal. To succeed and progress you must improve your skill, improve your fitness, and build experience. You can never master the sport because you can always find new water and new challenges.

This book tries to leave the real rewards of kayaking white water untouched and unmentioned. The aim is to help you to improve your performance, to understand water and its interaction with the kayak, and to cultivate positive attitudes to safety so that you can enhance your own special satisfaction from the sport.

Self-reliance and independence are fundamental to kayaking. They are qualities which must be brought to bear in deciding to paddle a rapid, choosing equipment, and in improving your skill. You must take responsibility for your own learning and follow these three simple guidelines:

1 Seek advice and guidance from experienced paddlers and coaches.
2 Read, ask questions, and discuss your paddling.
3 Know your limitations and weaknesses. Do not kid yourself that, because you have survived a Grade V rapid you are a Grade V paddler.

Finally, I would like to say that getting into a kayak and running rivers has nothing whatsoever to do with a person's sex or age. If you have a desire to paddle white water, then you have passed the only selection procedure in the sport. The clothing and equipment of kayaking remove much of your normal social identification. One group of paddlers looks very much the same as the next and you can be certain that you will never be treated more equally than when you launch out into a rapid.

Ray Rowe

CHAPTER 1

BOATS AND EQUIPMENT

Kayaks for use on white water vary considerably in their design and construction. This is because their application on the river might require a particular design characteristic to be emphasized. Some kayaks, for example, are designed specifically for touring long, wilderness rivers, while others are intended for jumping waterfalls. Most paddlers compromise in their choice of a kayak so that they can enjoy a little of everything that white-water paddling offers without having to own more than one boat. White-water kayak designs fit into the main categories described below.

HIGH-VOLUME TOURING KAYAKS

The term 'volume' refers to the amount of air enclosed by the entire kayak shell. These boats ride high on white water because of their volume, and this gives them a 'well-behaved', predictable feel. At lengths of up to 4 metres (13 feet), they are the longest of the white-water kayaks, and therefore are termed 'directional'; in other words, they hold a straight course, making direct lines through rapids very easy. Such kayaks are used on long river expeditions where the paddlers are carrying all of their equipment in the boats. Some very long descents of wilderness rivers throughout the world have been made in completely self-contained style by groups using high-volume kayaks. Beginners to white water can make fast progress through the degrees of difficulty using this kind of boat because the kayak feels stable in rough water and is not easily deflected from its course. It is possible to put the kayak in at the top of large, straight rapids and survive the run by keeping the boat nosing downhill. This kind of success must be treated with some caution because running a rapid and staying upright do not imply any degree of control and, sooner or later, a paddler who is out of control will pay the price.

MEDIUM VOLUME FOR GENERAL USE

By far the greatest number of kayaks used on white water fall into this category. They are usually between 330 and 370 centimetres (130 to 145 inches) long and 60 centimetres (24 inches) wide. Being shorter, these kayaks are much easier to turn, and the slightly lower decks give them a more snug fit around the paddler. The result is a machine which feels responsive and which transmits the energy of the river directly to the paddler. Because of this, it is an excellent boat design in which to learn and develop good white-water skills. Most of these kayaks are made in polyethylene which is a tough moulded plastic. Thus, a boat of this kind is a good investment for anyone.

LOW-VOLUME KAYAKS

Competition slalom-racing kayaks are made low in the decks to allow them to slide cleanly under the hanging gates. Other low-volume kayaks are built purely for fun and are called 'squirt boats'. They are shaped as flat as possible in cross-section and have sharply angled edges. The result is a boat which can submerge either end easily, especially its rear. A skilful paddler can perform many acrobatic manoeuvres by using the current, waves, and body rotation. The pivot turn is a simple example. This type of kayak has little or no space inside to carry equipment and is not suitable for beginners.

VERY SHORT KAYAKS

Many European white-water kayakers use a boat which looks very short to the uninitiated. To paddle one of these boats in a rapid is an experience not to be missed. The kayaks are about 220 centimetres (87 inches) long, and most have a fairly high-volume design. It is quite easy to stand the boat on its end,

and its short length makes controlling turning extremely easy. In middle-grade water, these kayaks are excellent fun boats, easy to eskimo roll and good for paddlers to use to improve their reactions. These short kayaks are taken much more seriously by some people, and they are used on extremely difficult water. Many alpine paddlers believe that they are the safest boats to use in Extreme White Water. As is always the case with equipment at this level, there are those who place great confidence in the unique characteristics of this particular machine while others disapprove. Undoubtedly, very short boats have a very low forward acceleration which causes problems in penetrating holes and waves, but they do have an uncanny knack of floating happily over the most formidable water. Some of the very steep sections of mountain rivers in Britain would simply not be possible without the use of a very short kayak.

A high-volume kayak which is suitable for extreme white-water paddling. It is constructed in fibreglass and diolene. *Length* 360 centimetres (142 inches). *Volume* 320 litres (under 11½ cubic feet).

A medium-volume kayak which is suitable for medium-grade white-water paddling. It is constructed from polyethylene. *Length* 355 centimetres (140 inches). *Volume* 250 litres (under 9 cubic feet).

A low-volume slalom competition kayak constructed from fibreglass and diolene. *Length* 400 centimetres (158 inches). *Volume* (just over 6½ cubic feet).

A very short kayak suitable for all levels of white-water paddling. It is constructed from polyethylene. *Length* 290 centimetres (114 inches). *Volume* 210 litres (under 7½ cubic feet).

CHOOSING YOUR BOAT

One factor which must influence your choice of kayak is your body weight and build. If you weigh between 10 and 12 stones (64 to 77 kilograms), a medium-volume boat will handle well for you. The same boat, with, say, a 14-stone (90-kilogram) paddler on board, will be slower to turn because so much more of its hull is in the water and it will generally handle more sluggishly. The heavier paddler must choose a boat with more volume. Naturally, this will also allow more room inside for larger feet and legs.

KAYAK CONSTRUCTION MATERIALS

Not too long ago all white-water kayaks were made up in two halves in moulds, like a chocolate Easter egg, and then joined together. They were made from fibreglass and resin or a refinement of these, and the result was very much a hand-made craft. Today, most white-water kayaks are made in an electronically heated mould from a plastic called polyethylene. In most cases, the mould is rotated to distribute the molten material, and very quickly a new boat is born. The simplicity of the manufacturing process and the incredible toughness of polyethylene has revitalized white-water kayaking. Boats last longer, and paddlers can afford to get afloat on to rivers in low water levels which would certainly have damaged fibreglass kayaks. The confidence gained from realizing that polyethylene kayaks could endure such wear and tear has led to a revolution of river exploration throughout the world.

Although polyethylene is extremely tough, it is also very pliant. A raw shell taken from the mould is quite floppy and, in most cases, an internal skeleton is fitted to give the kayak rigidity. This usually takes the form of plastic foam walls fitted centrally under the front and rear decks. These walls are clamped into place with bolts through the deck. Naturally, it is essential that these walls are strong and secure. An advantage of fibreglass compared to polyethylene is that it can be made resistant to bending without too much weight penalty. When it is finally bent, fibreglass will usually tear completely. This can be useful if a boat is pinned on a boulder, for example. Quite a few German kayakers still use fibreglass boats for these reasons.

OTHER BOAT FEATURES

Turning and speed through the water

The curve which a designer puts in the hull of a boat is called 'rocker'. The greater the amount of rocker,

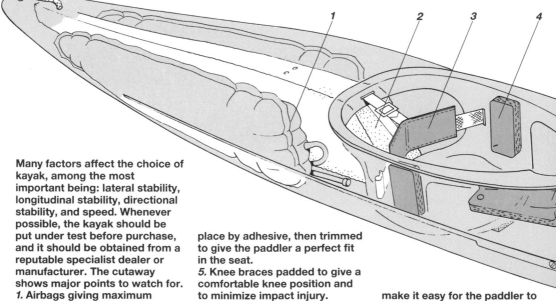

Many factors affect the choice of kayak, among the most important being: lateral stability, longitudinal stability, directional stability, and speed. Whenever possible, the kayak should be put under test before purchase, and it should be obtained from a reputable specialist dealer or manufacturer. The cutaway shows major points to watch for.
1. Airbags giving maximum flotation and additional strength to the deck and hull.
2. Rear foam wall which, in some kayaks, also functions as a back support.
3. Backstrap firmly secured.
4. Hip pads made from polythene foam and held in place by adhesive, then trimmed to give the paddler a perfect fit in the seat.
5. Knee braces padded to give a comfortable knee position and to minimize impact injury.
6. Full-plate footrest; the feet rest on a 3-inch (75-millimetre) thick block of polythene foam, providing impact absorption and warmth.
7. Buoyancy bags.
8. Front foam wall.
9. Safety cockpit designed to make it easy for the paddler to get out. It is longer than traditional kayak cockpits. The pronounced narrowing of the cockpit brings part of the thigh, as well as the knee, into contact with the boat.
10. Grab loop.
11. Toggle.

the easier it will be for the boat to spin with the paddler. Ultimately, this leads to a trade-off against the kayak's forward speed because increase in rocker means decrease in waterline length and therefore less speed in a straight line.

The cockpit area

Your only contact with the kayak is through the footrest and the cockpit area. If you are not comfortable and happy with the cockpit, you will not be happy with the kayak. The cockpit contains: the seat, the back support, the cockpit rim, and the knee or thigh braces.

Many modern cockpits are keyhole shaped. The shape results from making the cockpit long to allow easy escape and yet narrow to give purchase for the thighs. This large cockpit shape is often referred to as a 'safety cockpit'. Beginners in white water are often much happier in kayaks designed with safety cockpits, and many experienced paddlers prefer them. Practically every white-water kayak in Germany, Austria, and Switzerland is fitted with a keyhole-shaped safety cockpit because paddlers in the European Alps are very concerned about becoming trapped. Someone of average height can step out of a keyhole cockpit without lifting their backside off the seat first. In effect, this means that the paddler can leave the kayak without using the hands.

The knee braces provide the supports whereby you control the balance of the kayak. With your legs relaxed, you should feel contact with both knees on the braces. When keyhole-shaped cockpits were first introduced, paddlers felt that the large open space would make it difficult for them to gain firm purchase with their legs. In fact, most have come to realize that they have better kayak control with the thigh braces which are used in the safety cockpit.

With the keyhole cockpit, more of the leg is in contact with the boat. This brings the work of controlling boat balance closer to the pelvis, and the paddler can therefore exert more effort on the braces.

Back supports are very important in kayaking because they help you to lock yourself securely into the boat. If you sit on a kayak seat and push hard with both legs against the footrest your backside slips rearwards on the seat. The back support prevents this slackness and removes some tension from your groin. This tension is the result of using pressure on your knees to hold you in position when a back support is missing.

The back support is usually a webbing strap held securely above the seat and padded for comfort. Some adjustment of the back strap is needed to get the correct support position. Paddlers often fit their own backstraps *after* buying their kayaks. Remember two things:
1 The strap must be strong. If it

12. Grab handle, which is far superior to the others and should be capable of holding a minimum of 1100 pounds (500 kilograms) without breaking.

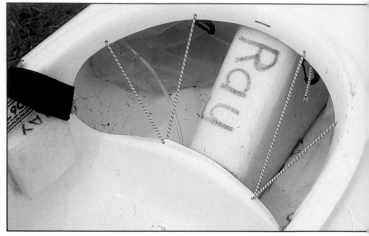

breaks when you are reversing you will shoot off the seat on to the rear cockpit rim;

2 It must be secured in tension so that it can not lift upwards and hinder your exit from the boat or drop downwards so that you sit on it when you get in.

Keyhole-shaped cockpits have a wide clearing between the back of the seat and the cockpit rim and so a backstrap is especially important with them. Some polyethylene

Above left: A full rear airbag.

Above right: This wall must be made from strong, non-brittle foam because it forms the internal skeleton of the kayak.

kayaks have a moulded flange on the rear of the seat into which the foam wall for the rear of the boat fits. In these boats the flange, and sometimes the foam wall itself, doubles

as the back support. Notice from the illustration that this cockpit area is split in front of the seat by the front foam wall. This wall gives superb support around the paddler's legs, for example, and also forms a back-up knee brace should a knee slip off the plastic moulded brace. A slip like this can occur when a paddler is working hard in heavy water. This kind of security, however, must be traded off against the impedance to the paddler's legs by the foam

---

KAYAK FLOTATION

The purpose of internal flotation is to exclude water. Airbags tailored to fit alongside the foam walls do the job very well. The fabric and construction of the bags and tubes need to be strong and capable of

withstanding increase in pressure. Inflating bags to slightly less than 'rock' hard gives you a little leeway if there is serious compression exerted on them. The airbags can be deflated partially to allow gear to be carried.

The gear is securely held in place by the tension of the re-inflated bag. Airbags must be secured into the kayak. Joining them with cord through a small hole in the foam wall is one way to do this.

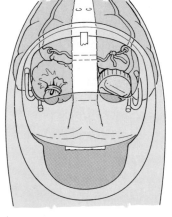

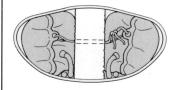

wall when he or she wants to leave the cockpit.

Finally, the seat sides must be made to fit the paddler. Manufacturers build these wide so that people of a variety of shapes can get their hips into the seat area. As a result, many paddlers find a space between their hips and the seat sides. You must take up this space with foam padding so that your hips rest comfortably in contact with the sides of the seat. This allows you to transmit movements of your pelvis directly to the kayak. It is best to build the sides up using non-absorbent foam layers held in place by a waterproof adhesive. While you are doing that, you will find it useful to line the knee braces with a thin piece of foam for comfort. If your knees are loose on the braces you can also build the braces downwards with layers of foam.

Kayak flotation

A kayak without any flotation attached to it will sink when water is allowed to enter the cockpit. Manufacturers build flotation into boats to prevent this. This flotation comes in two forms:
1 The foam walls, as used in this polyethylene kayak;
2 Airbags, as used in this Swiss fibreglass kayak.

When a kayak is allowed to swamp, it sinks into the water until it is supported by the flotation inside. If you have capsized and you are swimming with your kayak in a rapid, the swamped boat takes on the weight of the water inside, as well as its own weight. This could easily amount to 180 kilograms (400 pounds) and that, moving at say 8 miles an hour (13 kilometres an hour), represents a formidable amount of momentum. Apart from the injury this could cause if it hit you, this is the weight which you have to drag to the river bank. So it makes sense to fill every space in the kayak with flotation and exclude water from everywhere but the cockpit area.

Airbags fitted alongside foam walls are a superb form of additional flotation, and they have the advantage of allowing equipment to be held securely against the walls. Air-

FOOTRESTS

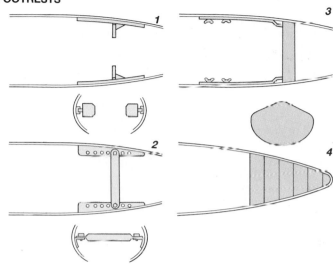

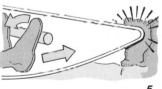

1. The adjustable pedal footrest is comfortable but lacks shock-absorbing properties.

2. Traditional bar system. It is mounted on flanges for adjusting.

3. Full-plate system with adjuster bolts near cockpit.

4. Bulkhead formed by solid foam plug filling the front space.

5. The rotation of the foot around a bar footrest during impact. This can cause damage to the ankle.

bags, particularly strong ones, give enormous support to a boat's decks in the event of it being held against an obstruction in a rapid. The fact that the swamped kayak floats much higher also reduces its chances of suffering damage or bending on obstructions, such as stakes or bridge piers. The boat floats higher so the water has less purchase on it. It is important that airbags are held securely in place because the pressure of water on a swamped kayak often squeezes them into the cockpit area. A well-secured backstrap holds them in nicely but it is useful to tie the airbags off as well.

Footrests

No kayaker should ever contemplate going on white water without a footrest. It is essential to help the paddler control the boat, to hold him

or her securely in the cockpit, and it also prevents the kayaker disappearing under the front deck if the front hits an obstruction. You should adjust the footrest until your legs are being held with knees apart and in contact with the braces. It is worth spending time to get the right footrest system. The footrest can be compared to running shoes. It is the point through which you deliver most of your paddling impulse and it must absorb shock.

The bar footrest supports the ball of the foot only and, if the front of the kayak collides with anything, the ankle joint compresses. This can cause extremely painful ligament damage to the ankle.

The plate system supports the whole foot and greatly reduces the risk of injury of this kind. The plate also has a foam pad on its face which functions as a shock absorber. This is the kind of footrest used in waterfall jumping where the paddler might fall directly on to rock and place huge loads on the footrest.

The bulkhead footrest is glued or bolted permanently in position. It is usually a solid wall of foam blocks built to fit the paddler exactly. It is a heavy system but it is also the safest and most secure.

The pedal footrest system is used by a lot of manufacturers. It is very comfortable, easy to adjust, and places the paddler's feet correctly on the sides of the boat and not in the middle. The only serious failing with the pedal footrest system is its lack of a shock-absorbing element.

Grab handles

The kayak's grab handle is an important link in the chain of equipment for safety. A swimmer in a rapid holds the kayak by the grab handle and, if a kayaker is trapped on an obstruction, rescuers use the grab handle to pull the kayaker free. The grab handle must be:
- strong [capable of holding 500 kilograms (1,100 pounds)];
- holdable [minimum of 10-millimetre (0.4-inch) diameter rope];
- escape-proof [not able to snag hands or fingers];
- at the end of the boat.

Loops can twist and crush fingers, although using very thick rope minimizes the risk. The only advantage of loops is that they can easily be replaced when worn so that a strength is maintained.

Toggles are excellent for holding on to a boat in rough water but their attachment to the boat must be equally strong. Toggles make it difficult to clip a rope on in a rescue situation.

The grab handle has the advantage of standing clear of the boat and yet not trapping fingers. A karabiner clip can be attached easily. Grab handles mounted to fibreglass kayaks, however, are extremely difficult to replace. This places their strength in question after two years or so. Many kayakers in Britain and Europe fit deck lines to their kayaks to extend the grab handle principle even more.

Deck lines have the following advantages:

- Give a grab point along the whole length of the boat. Helpful to both swimmers and rescuers trying to make contact with a wet and slippery boat.
- Extremely useful for handling the kayak in awkward situations off the river, such as passing it up or down a steep bank.
- Useful for helping a swimmer climb on to the deck for rescue or river-crossing purposes.

The main argument against deck lines is that they can snag trees and branches in the river and actually create problems. This can easily be overcome by ensuring that the deck lines remain in tension on the deck, or even by having the manufacturer build a recess into the deck to take the rope. It is absolutely essential that continuous decklines, running along the edge of the cockpit, are not used. Decklines of this kind will certainly create problems.

CARRYING THE KAYAK

For very short distances the kayak is most conveniently carried like a suitcase, at its balance point at the cockpit rim. The exact point of balance is usually just in front of the seat support, giving a reasonable handle. For longer carries, or where you are walking over rough ground, it is much better to lift the boat on to one shoulder, again on its balance point at the cockpit. This brings it clear of your legs, making it easier to

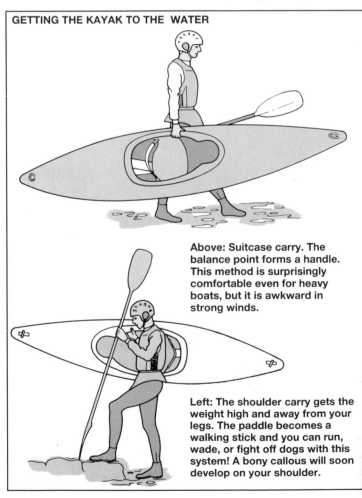

GETTING THE KAYAK TO THE WATER

Above: Suitcase carry. The balance point forms a handle. This method is surprisingly comfortable even for heavy boats, but it is awkward in strong winds.

Left: The shoulder carry gets the weight high and away from your legs. The paddle becomes a walking stick and you can run, wade, or fight off dogs with this system! A bony callous will soon develop on your shoulder.

step over boulders and climb on steep ground.

It is possible, of course, to double up with a partner to carry an end each of a single boat or the ends of both boats together. While this method makes it easier to bear the weight, it is more clumsy on difficult terrain and somehow detracts from the feeling of self-reliance which is fundamental to the sport. It would be foolish to attempt to lift a kayak heavily laden with camping gear on your own and, under these circumstances, getting help is essential if you are to avoid a back strain.

If you are alone and for some reason cannot lift your boat, you can always sledge it. Unless you are on grass or heather, take it slowly

The shoulder carry. This kayak weighs 19 kilograms (42 pounds). Such a considerable weight is most easily carried on the shoulders. Firstly, pick up the boat like a suitcase; then lift it and roll the opposite cockpit rim on to the shoulder.

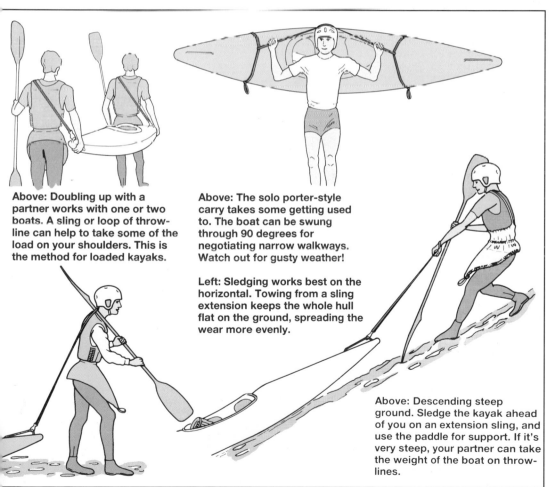

Above: Doubling up with a partner works with one or two boats. A sling or loop of throw-line can help to take some of the load on your shoulders. This is the method for loaded kayaks.

Above: The solo porter-style carry takes some getting used to. The boat can be swung through 90 degrees for negotiating narrow walkways. Watch out for gusty weather!

Left: Sledging works best on the horizontal. Towing from a sling extension keeps the whole hull flat on the ground, spreading the wear more evenly.

Above: Descending steep ground. Sledge the kayak ahead of you on an extension sling, and use the paddle for support. If it's very steep, your partner can take the weight of the boat on throw-lines.

This long carry into the mountains was made using the head strap carrying system. Your neck will take a while to get used to it.

because the abrasion on the kayak's hull can be considerable. Clipping your sling or shortened throw-line to the leading end of the boat makes a long haul easier especially if it is uphill. The same idea works for descending steep ground except that the sling functions like a dog leash clipped to the rear of the boat leaving the space in front of your feet clear for you to gain purchase. When the ground is steep and slippery for a long way, however, you should not hesitate to clip the kayak to your throw-line, and hoist or lower it separately.

Another solo-carry method which I have used for long walks into the mountains is to attach a lengthwise sling across the cockpit opening and to take the weight of the boat on my head. Once you get used to this method, and with the head strap well padded, it is a reasonably comfortable way to move.

At least half of the damage done to kayaks occurs when they are transported on vehicle roofs. Boats which have not been secured well enough are sometimes completely written off after being 'launched' involuntarily from car roofracks. Apart from the damage to the boat, the danger which flying kayaks present to pedestrians and other motorists is obvious. It is also quite common to see kayaks which have been well secured lifted from the roof crumpled and crushed through

overtightening of securing ropes. Polyethylene boats, particularly in warm weather, develop two depressions in their hulls to match the roofrack supports. There is no easy answer to the problem because the overriding priority must be security of the load on the roof for the safety reasons already mentioned.

Here are a few simple guidelines:
1 Use the strongest roofrack you can buy.
2 Use only strong rope or tape to secure boats.
3 Learn to tie reliable knots or, if you cannot, use tape straps with self-locking buckles.
4 Contoured kayak supports which bolt on to the roofrack considerably, reduce damage and are quicker to load.
5 Tie off the kayak ends to the car front and rear so that, if you do have

an accident, you are not relying on the roofrack clamps alone to restrain the load.

6 Seal off the cockpits on long journeys or in rain. You already know what an even partially water-logged boat weighs!

7 Do not leave anything, such as sponges, airbags, vacuum flasks, or throw-bags, unsecured inside the boats on the roof. Either the wind or souvenir hunters will remove them. It is possible to purchase a lock for your boat. This is a wire loop which goes around the seat support with an end which clamps inside the car door.

Many paddlers travel by air, taking their kayaks as baggage. Most of the large passenger aircraft can easily take a kayak in their holds even though some baggage handlers do not appear too keen on the idea. It has become a widely accepted ploy that you arrive at the check-in desk with your kayak at your side without any previous warning. Because it is easier for the check-in clerk to say 'yes' rather than 'no' most people get away with it and often, to their amazement, do not have to pay for the excess weight. My own experience has taught me to check the baggage stubs which are stapled to the ticket to see that the destination written on them is correct.

CARRYING KAYAKS ON ROOF RACKS

A kayak travels reasonably well sitting on its deck or hull. The securing rope or tape should be firm but not over-tight when it is attached to the kayak.

Use self-gripping buckles or good knots and a strong, solid roof rack. J-bars or back-to-back tying lets the boats travel on edge.

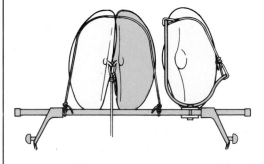

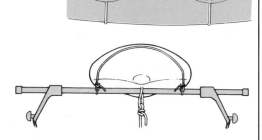

PERSONAL FLOTATION

White-water kayakers wear personal flotation (buoyancy aids) for two equally important reasons. In the event of taking a swim in a rapid, the jacket floats you high on the surface of the aerated water which would otherwise give little support to your body weight. The second reason is to give protection to your upper body against abrasion and impact with rock. Therefore, your buoyancy aid will have its closed-cell foam flotation distributed on the back and sides as well as on the front. The shape and construction of the jacket must allow you to perform freely the twisting and leaning trunk movements that are the essence of white-water paddling technique. Head movements and visibility must also be totally unobstructed.

The amount of flotation within a buoyancy aid is important to a paddler because this will determine how easy it is for you to keep your head above water if you go swimming in the waves and turbulence of a rapid. The International Canoe Federation stipulates that all competitors must wear a buoyancy aid containing 6 kilograms (13.2 pounds) of flotation in competitions on white water. That is to say, the flotation device must be capable of giving 6 kilograms of uplift in water. This is a minimum figure and barely adequate for a kayaker contemplating serious white water. A flotation of 9 to 10 kilograms (20-22 pounds) is much more realistic, because an exhausted swimmer needs every little piece of flotation there is to help

Top: This buoyancy aid contains 10 kilograms (22 pounds) of flotation. The chest strap is primarily part of the integral chest harness system but it also helps to mould the flotation foam to the torso.

Bottom: The buoyancy aid is secured around the waist by a tape and a quick-release buckle. This is better than the more common drawcord which can easily come undone.

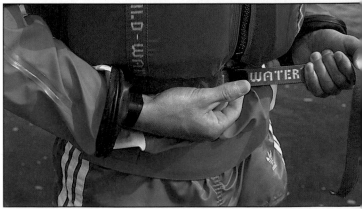

him or her survive a swim in white water at this level. Wearing a wetsuit can give another 4 kilograms (9 pounds) of flotation.

The trouble with increasing the jacket's flotation is that there is also an increase in bulk. This in turn becomes a hindrance to the paddler's movements in the boat. A flotation of 10 kilograms (22 pounds), using conventional closed-cell foam, would be the most that paddlers of average build can cope with.

Secondary functions of the buoyancy aid are:
• To insulate the trunk from cold
• To provide purchase for rescuers trying to grab the paddler.
• To hold simple safety equipment, such as a penknife.

Some buoyancy jackets are zipped to make them easy to put on, while others are simple vests which are pulled over the head. The constant hauling on and off stresses the stitching in the second type but, so long as this is kept in check, it is a perfectly good system.

Wearing the Jacket

The buoyancy aid is best worn as the outermost garment. It is essential that it fits you snugly and that there is no slackness under the arms or around the chest. The waist of the jacket should be secured firmly so that it cannot become undone accidentally. The security of fit of your buoyancy aid cannot be overemphasized, and you should practise swimming in yours to ensure that you have got it right. Jackets which have carefully positioned tensioning straps enable you to mould the vest to your own body shape. A tape and buckle around the waist is much more positive than nylon cord.

Finally, the white-water paddler's buoyancy aid should have nothing hanging from it that might fill with water or catch on trees or branches. It should be as neat and streamlined as its flotation will allow.

Old age

Every known synthetic material degrades naturally from the beginning of its life. The flotation in your buoyancy aid is no exception, and closed foam cells collapse at a rate of approximately 3 per cent a year. Therefore, it is worth replacing your buoyancy aid about every three years if you care about its ability to support you in water.

THE HELMET

A good white-water kayaking helmet should:
• Protect the front of the head and the temples.
• Be made of a strong material in the shell, able to withstand impact both on and off the river. For example, a thick polypropylene or polyethylene shell.
• Be a good fit on your head; it should grip your head all round so that there is no movement sideways or up and down.
• Have a foam liner to reduce the force of impact transmitted to the skull.
• Have a strong harness to hold it in place.

When a paddler capsizes, there is obviously a moment when the head is the part of the body nearest the river bed. Therefore, it is not at all uncommon for paddlers' heads to make contact with the rock or gravel of the river bed. A good helmet will allow you to do this without any further problems.

As you can see from the list of requirements it is not enough to wear a well-designed helmet – it must also fit your head perfectly. This sometimes requires trying many different types of helmet. The dimensions of human heads vary widely, and it is a designer's nightmare to create a cradle system which will fit all heads. If you have a helmet with a liner which cradles your skull, you might have to glue in pieces of foam and then trim them with a scalpel to achieve the perfect fit. Time taken on this kind of preparation is time well spent.

Many kayaking helmets have holes moulded into them. If you are paddling a warm river in hot weather you will be glad of the holes for ventilation. Otherwise, the holes merely weaken the helmet shell and help you to get cold. Holes should not be required for drainage purposes because water should not get

Poor head covering. The temples are completely exposed because the cradle inside the helmet, and the shell shape, prevent it from sitting on the head properly.

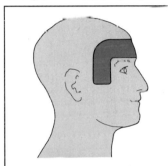

The frontal areas of the head and the nose are the most common sites of injury.

Good head covering. The temples are well protected and the helmet stands proud of the forehead, helping to protect the bridge of the nose.

into the perfectly fitting helmet in the first place. If it's winter and cold – tape up the holes and have a warm head.

It is important that you can hear when you are wearing a helmet. You can learn a lot about what is coming up next on the river by using your ears. The helmet should allow you to hear reasonably normally, although one German helmet has the luxury of hearing shutters.

Chin cups

I would suggest that you do not use a chin cup on your helmet because tests have shown that they alter the angle of pull of the chinstrap, so that it becomes easier for the helmet to slide backwards off your head. Your chinstrap should run parallel to the upward-pointing part of your jaw bone. A chin cup can slip off the chin and move upwards causing serious obstruction to the mouth.

Some helmets have a stability strap which runs from the rear, mid-point of the helmet to the chinstrap crossing under the ear. This is intended to prevent forward and rear-ward movement of the helmet and to reduce rotational slackness. It is very important that the attachment to the chinstrap is secure and not, as in some canoeing helmets, a piece of thin polythene. You can easily reinforce this yourself by having it stitched.

THE SPRAY DECK

Once again, the spray deck is a piece of equipment which directly affects your safety and your comfort. It keeps the water out and warmth in. It must stay in place under the considerable weight of water that can fall on it and yet it

---

SPRAY DECKS

Different edge seals.
Elastic rope is threaded into a sleeve made by a rolled-over seam in the skirt.
The elastic rope is stitched directly on to the skirt.

A rubber band is glued to the skirt giving a powerful grip on the cockpit rim.

Below: Parts of the spray deck.

Below: Anti-implosion bar stitched into the spray deck and spanning the cockpit rim.

Body tube

Skirt

Release strap

RELEASE STRAPS

Below: The best position for the release strap is at the apex.

Below: The tape should be stitched to the underside of the skirt so that it unrolls when pulled.

Below: A tape loop is the best system when hands are numb with cold.

Left: Use two movements to remove the spray deck. Pull forwards and then upwards. It will last longer and come off easier if you do.

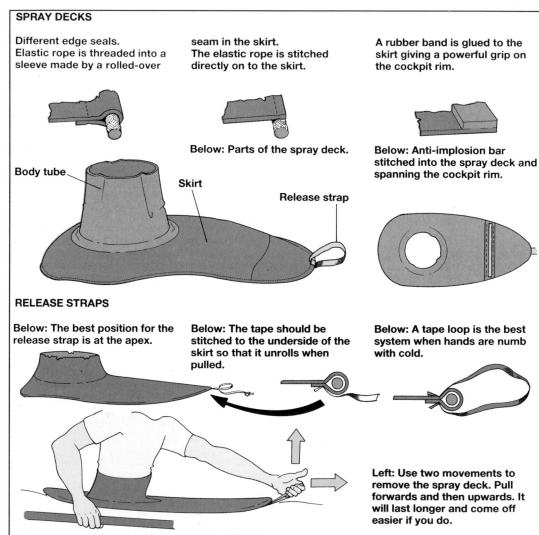

must be easily removable in emergencies. This is a tall order, and the secret lies in the materials used.

Neoprene, the synthetic rubber from which wetsuits are made, is the most successful material from which spray decks have been made. The natural tension in the material prevents the skirt from sagging with water while it is stretched on to the cockpit rim, and the neoprene body tube flexes and stretches with the paddler's upper body movements. A good-quality neoprene spray deck is constructed with 'blind seams', that is, the seams are completely waterproof. This is a necessity if you plan to paddle long stretches of heavy water.

The skirt is secured to the cockpit rim by one of three systems shown in the illustrations. For durability the first system is hard to beat because you can always rethread broken elastic rope into the sleeve. The third method undoubtedly creates the most watertight seal on the cockpit rim and is especially good on polyethylene boats which are notoriously difficult to seal.

This spray deck grips the cockpit extremely tightly, making it implosion proof and able to withstand 'blow-off'. This occurs when water compresses the kayak, which causes air pressure from within to drive the spray deck off outwards. It is a very common reason for spray deck failure in heavy water. Being swamped in the middle of a rapid because of it can bring about a sense-of-humour failure in all but the most relaxed of paddlers!

Some spray decks are fitted with an anti-implosion bar. This spans the cockpit rim and helps prevent the skirt from collapsing, especially in the case of a safety cockpit. The bar is, however, sometimes a hindrance while swimming, and there is always the possible risk that it might

get caught between rocks.

Good-quality spray decks have a very strong grip on the cockpit rim, and often they can only be released by a positive tug on the *release strap*. Release straps come in various forms. One is a loop of tape stitched into the front of the skirt. A single tape knotted or with a toggle attached does the same job. Another system is to use the elastic rope which secures the skirt extended out of its sleeve at the front and knotted to give a handle. What is important about the release strap is that it is attached firmly to the skirt so that it will not be pulled off in an emergency. The tape should be sewn to the underside of the skirt so that it causes the skirt to

roll off the cockpit rim when it is pulled. Develop the habit of using a 'pull and lift' action on the release strap. This places less strain on the stitching and reduces wear on the edge of the skirt.

CLOTHING

Many white-water accidents have either been caused by or resulted in the casualty suffering from hypothermia. This is a clinical condition caused by a fall in the body's temperature and the results can be debilitating or even fatal.

The body's inability to maintain its healthy working temperature can be brought on by exhaustion and gradual cooling over a period of hours

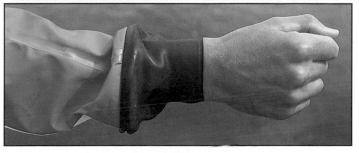

Top: The paddling cag is tailored to allow you to work unrestricted with your arms above your head.

Bottom: A 'dry-seal' cuff. Handle such cuffs carefully because they can tear easily.

or it can be as a result of sudden profound cooling in the case of immersion in very cold water. Both types of hypothermia can occur in white-water kayaking, but it is immersion cooling which takes by far the heaviest toll of paddlers. In a long swim in, say, snow meltwater which is only just above freezing point, a paddler can be quickly rendered unconscious by the rapid cooling of the body. Therefore every white-water kayaker should think carefully about the clothing system to be worn for a particular trip.

The 'cag'

The kayaking jacket or 'cag' forms a windproof barrier for the upper body. It must be flexible and cut correctly in the sleeves to allow the paddler to work freely with arms above the head. The cag should be as waterproof as possible. The most expensive have latex drysuit seals at the neck and cuffs, while cheaper models have neoprene seals. The neoprene works well enough because it is a good insulator and has enough tension to exclude most of the water. The waterproof fabric of the garment needs to be of good quality because of the wear and tear which will quickly destroy cheap proofing. Neoprene-proofed 150-gram (6-ounce) nylon is a reasonable fabric to use in a cag. Make sure the cuffs fit you well and, if the neck seal is too large, add velcro so that you can close it down securely on those particularly cold days.

The wetsuit and drysuit

Under the cag, comes the spray deck and then the next layer of clothing. If there is any possibility of a cold-water swim then a wetsuit is the most practical way of safeguarding your body heat. The wetsuit provides insulation against cold water, is buoyant, and protects the paddler's legs and hips from abrasion when wading or swimming in shallow water. Kayakers usually prefer to use sleeveless wetsuits about 3 millimetres (0.12 inch) thick. This is the thin end of the range of neoprene and is chosen because it offers little restriction to body movement. Many paddlers in Germany and Austria still use wetsuits with

full-length sleeves in winter and early spring, and the improvement in quality of modern neoprene will be a great help to these brave souls.

If you decide to use a sleeveless wetsuit, your choice of clothing to wear with it is much more important, especially if your cag is not totally waterproof. Polypropylene underwear is ideal to wear below a wetsuit because it is very thin and elastic. The individual fibres of plastic which make up the fabric do not soak up water and so it remains light and non-sagging when it gets wet. The material dries simply by draining downwards under gravity and this reduces body heat loss through evaporation. Polypropylene makes very compact clothing so it is easy to carry spare layers to improve

Right: A sleeveless wetsuit made from 3-millimetre (0.12-inch) neoprene. These are popular with white-water paddlers.

Below: A polypropylene vest. This is ideal kayak wear. The fabric is very elastic; it does not hang from the arms when it is wet; and it dries fast. When it has been worn for a few weeks, it takes on a unique fragrance. In winter, a fibrepile or light woollen sweater can be worn on top of the vest.

insulation as you go along. Other synthetic materials, such as polyester, are made into fabrics which give greater insulation. Fibre pile and synthetic fleece are examples of these more bulky materials which are excellent for paddling in cold weather. They are quick to dry and, like all synthetic clothing, are durable, a crucial quality in paddlers' clothing.

Full-body drysuits are also used in white-water paddling, especially when the paddlers are moving around in low air temperatures out of their kayaks. It is essential that all the air is vented from these suits before setting off because air trapped in the legs can hinder a swimmer in a rapid. A drysuit is very comfortable to paddle in, but it makes it difficult to urinate during a trip. The seals at the wrist, neck, and ankles of a drysuit are quite delicate and require a lot of care in handling so that they do not tear.

The clothing worn under the drysuit remains mostly dry apart from a little moisture accumulated through sweating. Lightweight, low-bulk clothing in amounts proportional to the temperature of the water and air can be worn. One of the really good things about drysuits is the way they prevent wind chill.

Wool and cotton clothing

Cotton is largely inappropriate for use in white-water clothing because it is a very poor insulator when it is wet. It draws heat from your body to dry itself and it quickly degrades and rots with constant soaking.

Wool, however, is a natural fabric which should not be discounted by the kayaker. Although it is bulky and slow to dry, wool has excellent insulation properties, which it barely loses when it becomes wet. Many past seafarers owe their survival

A full drysuit. This is excellent winter wear. The neck, wrists, and ankles have light rubber seals. Attached socks should not be used for kayaking in case water enters the suit accidentally. This type of suit is put on by means of a waterproof zip across the shoulders.

from long periods in wet clothing to the high insulation of wool. Thin woollen underwear worn inside a wetsuit is a delight in cold weather. Woollen yarns containing very fine-quality fibres do not cause the skin irritation which people often complain about. Underwear made from wool and polypropylene mixtures offers a good blend of the hard-wearing, shape-retaining qualities of synthetics and the warmth and softness of wool.

Footwear

Paddling wild rivers involves an incredible amount of running on roads, climbing scree and rock, and ploughing through mud. There is no substitute for a good solid pair of wetsuit boots. A pair with a tough moulded boot bonded to a neoprene sock is about the best you can have. The boot protects your feet if you have to scrabble along the river bed after a swamped boat, is comfortable for 10-mile (16-kilometre) runs on roads to pick up transport, and yet flexible enough to use effectively in a swim.

The traditional kayaker's footwear of wetsuit socks inside one-size-over, worn-out trainers is great for the image but can let you down at awkward moments.

Hands

Kayakers must retain skin contact with the paddle shaft for 'feel'. The successful equipment covers the back of the hand but leaves the inside free. For really cold climates, insulated mitts are excellent. Various kinds of lightweight synthetic insulation are used to bond to the inside of the mitt.

Right: Wetsuit boots with bonded socks. The moulded rubber boot gives good protection to the feet and, in snow-melt rivers or in winter paddling, the high insulation they afford is essential. Such boots are much more reliable than the traditional kayaker's footwear. At the campsite on a windless night, sit close to your drying wetsuit boots and you'll discover a new world of aromas!

Above: Paddle mitts, as worn by today's white-water kayaker. They cover the back of the hands for warmth and protection but the hands still have 'feel'.

Right: These paddle mitts are lined with insulating material. They are superb in freezing weather. Various synthetics are used to provide insulation.

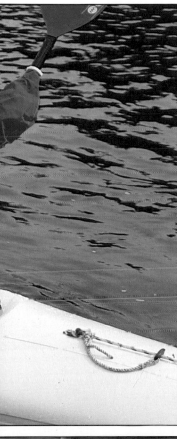

PADDLES

A white-water kayak paddle must conform to the following requirements. It must:
- Have strong blades capable of being crashed against rocks, especially on its edges.
- Have a strong shaft which the paddler can use to support his or her weight.
- Have ovalled grips at the hand positions on the shaft.

- Be free of sharp edges and corners on the blades which can snag between rocks or in crevices.

Shallow, rocky rivers are usual for most white-water paddlers, so the paddles must be capable of taking the severe punishment which this kind of river inflicts on them. Many alpine and British mountain rivers require the paddler to use rock rather than water for bracing on. As a result, the most successful paddle construction has been the compo-

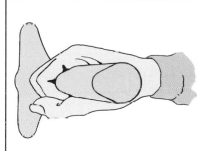

OVALLED GRIPS

An ovalled shaft or moulded grip is absolutely essential for paddles which are to be used in white water. It is especially important on the control-hand side, because it allows you to lock your hand into the correct position on the shaft without the need to look.

Below: Kayak paddles. *From left to right:* composite white-water paddle; wooden paddle; asymmetric racing paddle; economy white-water paddle, fibreglass blade and alloy shaft. These paddles conform with the requirements for white-water use. They have strong blades and shafts to withstand the punishment they are bound to be subjected to. The ovalled grip found on good paddles is shown in the diagram above.

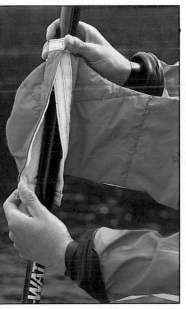

site blade with an alloy shaft. These blades are a glass-reinforced plastic mixture baked on to an alloy frame. The whole paddle is exceptionally strong and, although it is heavier than most other types of construction, its strength gives confidence to the paddler. Kayakers paddling in deep, white-water rivers can afford to use lighter paddles with fibreglass or carbon-fibre blades and shafts. Wooden paddles are warm, springy, and a delight to use but require more maintenance.

The blades of white-water paddles are usually curved along their length to give purchase on the water. Curving across the blades, or spooning, gives better purchase but poses problems when the blade slices sideways. This is a common paddle movement and a spoon blade tends to slice in a curve or arc which is usually not part of the plan!

There is a rule-of-thumb to help you decide what length your paddle should be. Stand the paddle up. You should be just able to curl your fingers around the edge of the top blade. You will know very quickly if your paddle is the wrong length. Too long a shaft will cause the blades to work too deeply and it will be awkward to lift them clear of the water. Your stroke rate in forward paddling will be slow. Too short a shaft simply prevents you from using all of the blade in the water.

CARRYING EQUIPMENT

The kinds of things which you might carry in your kayak range from a camera to camping equipment and food for an extended trip. The boat will only hold about the same amount as you can get into a large mountain expedition rucksack so you must be careful in your choice of equipment.

Keeping things dry is the big challenge and there are two main kinds of storage.
1 Rigid or semi-rigid plastic con-

To ensure that your paddle is the correct length, stand it up beside you – you should be able to curl your fingers around the top of the blade.

tainers with watertight lids. These come in all shapes and sizes. They are usually very durable and are especially useful for carrying particularly delicate items, such as cameras, film, fibreglass repair kits, or medical supplies.

2 Waterproof bags. Clothing, tents, and sleeping bags fit well into these and give a long flexible shape which can be winkled into spaces around the kayak. Several small bags are more useful than one large one for distributing weight. Nylon bags fitted with polythene liners and secured with rubber bands or cord is a good, cheap method, while more expensive bags of good-quality fabric with quick closures speed up packing by their very simplicity.

It is important to mark or colour-code your bags and containers so that it is easy to find dry clothes, or food, or a first-aid kit. A combination of soft gear bags and polythene bottles is a good system.

The boat should be packed so that heavy items, such as stoves and fuel, are close to the cockpit. This keeps weight away from the ends and makes handling the heavy kayak a little easier. The cockpit area must be left free and it is important to secure gear into the boat. Meshing off the whole rear of the cockpit is the only sure way of keeping things in the rear of the boat.

Equipment stored behind a foot-rest plate in the front is obviously very secure. Give some thought to the trim of the boat as you pack and, if you have to tip one way, then trim stern-low rather than bow-low.

Never allow anyone else to carry your dry clothing or sleeping bag (unless you have raft support), and remember that, although your boat feels very sluggish under the extra weight of all those bags, they also add to the internal flotation because they are airtight and they will help to exclude water if you do capsize.

REPAIRING YOUR KAYAK

One of the main shortcomings of the modern polyethylene kayak is that it is extremely difficult to make a satisfactory repair once the main shell has been holed. Most manufacturers have developed systems

CARRYING EQUIPMENT

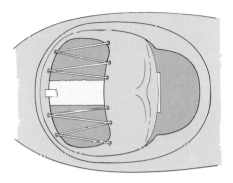

Above: Roping off the rear of the cockpit area helps keep the airbags in place and prevents the equipment from being lost. Nylon or elastic cord threaded through small holes drilled through the seat and cockpit edges does the job. Experiment with the equipment you have, but try to keep it simple.

Above: Waterproof containers. Soft nylon bags with polythene liners are the most popular. They can be winkled into spaces.

Above: Solid plastic containers protect cameras well and pad sharp objects like stoves.

for producing extremely robust plastic for their kayaks which is *almost* unbreakable. This is especially true of kayaks constructed by vacuum moulding which produces a very hard and slippery shell. The boat may still be holed if it is sliced by a very sharp reef of rock or as a result of any weaknesses which occur as the material degrades naturally with age or exposure to sunlight. Fibreglass kayaks, on the other hand, can easily be repaired using a resin-impregnated patch. This kind of repair work, however, must be carried out in a dry, warm atmosphere.

Short-term repairs to kayaks on the river bank are carried out with the famous 'canoe tape'. Like many other paddlers, I have used canoe tape to stop leaks, repair paddle shafts, cover blisters, strap up wrists, and repair tent poles. It is an essential part of the kayaker's life. Persuading canoe tape to stick to a wet hull on a rainy day is another story, however, involving blow-lamps, driftwood fires, and frantic massage of the afflicted area. A less aesthetically pleasing but extremely effective alternative is to use a mastic-impregnated plumber's tape designed for temporary repairs to water pipes. A hole in the kayak can be plugged and covered inside and out by this non-hardening tape. It is not pleasant to handle but it does the job and is re-usable. I suspect it is inedible!

CHAPTER 2

UNDERSTANDING WHITE WATER

There is a tantalizing thrill in setting off on to a river which is completely new to you, and in unveiling the secrets around the bends in its rapids and through its gorges. On the other hand, the kayaker on familiar, local water discovers new waves, understands the energy hidden within the rapids, and learns the dramatic changes which are brought with a rise or fall in water level. In both cases, the kayak paddler in white water is an explorer. In the former he or she is a traveller, moving at the speed of the river, and using its power to take boat and paddler along its path. In the latter the kayaker is searching and probing to find new movements in the kayak, new skills and strengths, and new ways to channel the forces of the river to advantage.

Whatever your goal, paddling rapid rivers is compulsive and extremely exciting but to be successful in your exploration, you must use cunning and caution. The water of the river can be a deadly adversary, and you must tackle it properly equipped and with an understanding of its movements. If you cannot look at the water and read its waves and surges, then you have no basis on which to plan your tactics for paddling. If you have no plan then, you will enter the rapid and be taken by the water and you might just as well have climbed into a barrel and asked someone to push you out into the current.

The water in a river behaves reasonably predictably whether it is tumbling off a mountainside or bowling along deep, wide channels. It is this predictability, combined with experience of water movement, which makes it possible for the paddler to read accurately an unfamiliar piece of river. It has been said that what lies beneath the waters of a rapid is written all over the surface. If you know something about the river bed, it will help you to know what kind of water formations to expect on the rapid.

The simplest formation of a rapid occurs when the current of a river is suddenly accelerated. This is usually brought about by a compression of the water through shallows or between boulders. It is sometimes seen downstream of a bridge where the water squirts out of the arches as though it were shooting from a hosepipe. The water in this formation takes on a characteristic appearance. The tongue of fast water forms a long 'V' which points downstream, and the still water on either side of it has a glass-like appearance. The still or slack water on either side of the 'V' is called an *eddy* and the line which forms the side of the 'V' is called the *eddy line*.

The 'V' shape on the rapid is usually very easy to see from the bank but needs practice to spot

Below: Looking down on a boulder field. This section is graded 4.

Right: Inspecting rapids. What you see; what others tell you; how you feel.

THE DOWNSTREAM 'V'

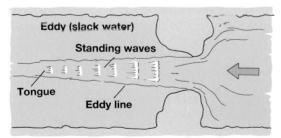

Eddy (slack water)

Standing waves

Tongue

Eddy line

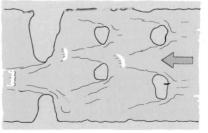

Above: A downstream 'V' formed by the acceleration of the current of the river by a single constriction. The still or slack water on either side of the 'V' is the eddy and has a glass-like appearance. Notice that the eddy line becomes less defined as it is followed downstream. Although it is usually easy to see downstream 'Vs' from the bank of the river, it is not so simple when you are actually on the water.

Above right: Downstream and upstream 'Vs' in a small boulder field create a simple 'street plan' showing the way for the paddler. Choose a route which makes it possible to connect 'V' shapes in sequence.

from the kayak. Recognizing these 'V' shapes is very important because they are the river's signposts showing you where the deep, clear channel is. Easy-grade rapids are well marked with a single 'V', and the kayaker has the simple task of broadly lining up the boat to allow it to slip through the middle of the tongue of water. More difficult rapids will have more than one 'V' showing, and you must choose a route which makes it possible to connect them in a sequence that will take you completely through the section. Water, which is even more difficult, presents you with a vast number of 'V' shapes, some of which are not clearly defined and have other river hazards waiting to pounce. You play a chess game of linked moves based on what you remember from inspecting the rapid beforehand and on how successful each individual move is.

WAVES

Notice that, within the 'V' of the simple rapid, a line of waves has formed. A wave is an expression of energy and, in this case, it has been provided by the surge of fast water hitting the more still pool of water beyond the constriction. These waves are *not* caused by water running over boulders, and they are called *standing waves*. They are closely related to the surf waves which land on the beach. Here the wave's energy has travelled from the middle of the ocean to the shore like a ripple sweeping across a blanket. In the river standing wave, the bump of the wave stands still and the water (or blanket) moves over it.

When a standing wave forms from a small amount of energy, it is a smooth, glassy hump like an ocean swell. If the same wave is given more energy by increasing the flow of water through it, the wave height increases until it reaches a critical height. This is the height beyond which the wave will break and tumble down its face. Thus, on any rapid, you will find solid, unbroken standing waves *and* steeper-sided waves with foaming and breaking crests. It is also common to find

Above: A paddler riding a huge standing wave on the River General in Costa Rica, Central America. The kayak points upstream and hurtles over the water rising towards the crest of the wave.

Left: Irregular standing waves on a Grade 3/4 stretch of the River Isére, France. Standing waves may be caused within a 'V' as the surge of fast water hits the quieter water.

Right: A procession of standing waves. Something of a 'roller-coaster' for the kayaker.

FORMATION OF A STANDING WAVE

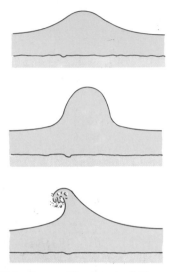

This river profile shows what happens to a standing wave as the volume of water increases. The initial small hump increases in height until it forms a continuous breaking wave.

FLAT-TOPPED WAVE

A paddler's-eye view approaching a standing wave.

HAYSTACK

The pyramid-shaped base and spraying top of a haystack.

ROOSTER TAIL

Side-on view of a rooster tail. Inside is a rock.

waves building their height, bursting at the top, and then starting to re-form all within a cycle of a few seconds. In tongues of fast water, standing waves align themselves downstream giving a superb roller-coaster ride to the paddler moving with the current.

Standing wave shapes

Seen from upstream, standing waves are either flat topped or pyramid shaped with broken tops spraying water like a fountain. The flat-topped waves can extend all the way across the river in some cases, such as when a sloping ledge causes an even drop in river level. The waves with broken tops are called 'haystacks'. This is because of their resemblance to the old hourglass-shaped stacks of hay in the fields. Haystacks are quite safe, fun, and a little wet to paddle over.

Rooster tail

Sharp-edged rocks pointing into the current may appear to be standing

Above: The calm water of the eddy alongside the fast white water of an alpine glacial river.

Left: At the top of the photograph is a rooster tail. From upstream, only the fan-shaped fountain can be seen. The rock in the middle of it is obvious from downstream!

Right: The flow of water falling over the rock forms a small 'hole'.

waves if they are covered by water. The paddler can sometimes see the rock showing through the water and the thin spray of water downstream also helps to pinpoint it. When the spray is pronounced and there is a pocket of air formed underneath it, the formation is known as a *'rooster tail'*.

Eddies

The calm water of an eddy responds to increases in energy levels in the river. As the strength of the current increases, so the eddy water is forced to move in the opposite direction to the stream. The clear-cut eddy line develops turbulence of its own as spiralling currents develop. These evolve into small whirl-pools of descending water and are accompanied by areas of *boils* (water rising to the surface). These conditions prevail where there is a large volume of water on the river. Exactly the same phenomenon can be seen in areas of strong tidal movement where the water is forced between islands or around bridges.

Irregularities on the river bed can also cause waves. A boulder near to the surface will form a small wave on its downstream side. The shaded pattern which this creates on the surface is called an *upstream 'V'*. Once again, a 'V', albeit much less well defined this time, works as a signpost. It indicates the rock below the surface and the kayaker knows to steer around it. With two sub-merged rocks close to each other, the route through the downstream 'V' is very clear.

If the boulder or obstruction extends above the surface then the water is deflected around it and a wave forms on the upstream side. This is called a *cushion wave*. If we look at the same boulder at different water levels, we can see why variations in level can have such a profound effect on the kayaking.

A large boulder covered by a high column of water develops a wave action on its downstream side which paddlers describe as a *hole*. A hole is exactly what it seems to be. There, directly behind the boulder, is a trough with water tumbling into it. The water in the hole is circulating. A paddler who goes over the top of the boulder drops deeply into it, often disappearing from sight for a moment. Large holes are quite capable of holding and tumbling a kayak and its paddler, and even small ones snatch the boat viciously. Unless you are working well within your limits you should always steer around them.

Stoppers or hydraulics

The recirculating water in a hole illustrates a water phenomenon which kayakers treat with great respect. Water falling into still water sets up a vertical eddy called a *stopper* or *hydraulic*. It is called a stopper because a kayak passing through the formation meets water moving towards it, that is, upstream. The grip of this on the boat and on the paddler's chest actually stops the boat and the paddler must use powerful paddle strokes to get through it. Stoppers fall broadly into two categories:

1 Those in which the circulation is mostly on the surface.

2 Those in which circulation extends deeply below the surface.

Surface stoppers are powerful

A larger 'hole' on the Zambezi river in southern Africa. The paddler has decided wisely to skirt around it. Good judgement is an important asset here.

UPSTREAM 'V'	DOWNSTREAM 'V'
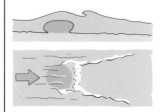	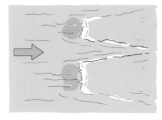
The partially covered boulder is 'signposted' by the 'V'.	Deep-water channel marked by downstream 'V'.

CUSHION WAVE

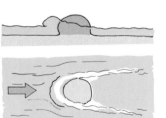

Cushion wave on the upstream side of a boulder.

RISING WATER FORMING A HOLE

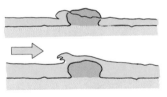

As the boulder becomes covered, water tumbling over it starts to recirculate, causing a hole which will attract boats to its grip. Wise kayakers always treat this kind of water with respect.

SURFACE CIRCULATION

A surface stopper forms when water deflected upwards descends at a shallow angle into deeper water. A white, cascading wave marks the spot. Just below the surface water is undisturbed.

DEEP CIRCULATION

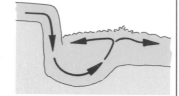

Here, the water plunges steeply into a deep pool creating a long tow-back. Deep circulating stoppers often occur on weirs and low head dams.

WEIRS

Weirs are constructed on rivers to regulate and control the flow of water. The backed-up water can be used to drive turbines, machinery at mills, or for irrigation. Most modern weirs are built of concrete and steel. Some engineers include a ledge near the base of the weir to reduce the scouring effect of the water on the river bed and therefore prolong the life of the river. These create horrific tow-backs and provide the added danger of trapping the nose of a kayak should it plunge deep

formations but below the turbulent, cascading surface is a solid and uninterrupted flow of water downstream. If you capsize in one of these, this lower current will drag you away and clear of the wave. A swimmer passes through the stopper because he or she is low in the water and will pass under the white circulating wave.

These formations are usually noisy and spectacular which give their position away to kayakers. It is in these that paddlers play by sitting broadside, ecstatically side-surfing the wave, not going anywhere yet experiencing a sensation of speed. These, too, will often pull in the end of a boat and shoot it out skywards.

Deep, circulating stoppers occur where water falls vertically into a deep plunge pool. They occur commonly on artificial structures, such as weirs or low head dams, and they have caused many kayakers to drown. The formation is characterized by a long tow-back of water moving towards the drop and bubbles, rather like boiling water, rising to the surface. As you can see from the illustration, the downstream escaping water is a long way below the surface and the paddler in the kayak has little chance of taking advantage of it. A swimmer, desperate to stay on the surface and get air, is held in the deadly circulation until exhausted.

It is usually difficult to give good rescue cover to a paddler contemplating such a piece of water and the risk to the rescuers is high. The only safe way to negotiate a deep stopper is to walk around it.

enough. In high-river conditions *all* weirs are dangerous to the kayaker. The difference in level of water above and below the weir bears no relation to the power of the stopper. Any weir which is questionable is not worth the trouble.

Right: This weir was roughly constructed using enormous blocks pushed into position. Remember that weirs can be very dangerous and if you are uncertain about one, leave it alone.

A SIDE-ON VIEW OF WEIR TYPES

Anti-scour sill at base of weir. This is a very difficult stopper and there is a risk of head injury.

Vertical weir. This is the worst of all for stopper danger at any level. If you must, go over at full speed.

Inclined and vertical. These tend to be high but the ramp gives a good take-off to clear the stopper.

Inclined weir. This type is usually safe in low to medium water but difficult in high water.

Curved weir. Shallow landing in low water. It is a serious stopper in high conditions.

Stepped weir. The steps are often formed by tanks which work as a fish pass. Watch out for stoppers in each tank step. This is a difficult rescue site!

Above: In this instance a paddler has chosen to ignore the downstream 'V' and ride directly through the stopper.

Left: A surface stopper. This one is caused by a smooth ledge of rock stretching across the river. A safe channel past the stopper is signposted by the 'V'.

Right: A deep circulating stopper. The water is quietly surging towards the weir.

INSPECTING RAPIDS

Unless you know a rapid to be very straightforward, you should get out of the boat and look at it from the bank before attempting to run it. There are three sources of information when you do this:

1 What you see – you relate this to your past experience of white water and your understanding of river movement.

2 What other kayakers tell you – information about others' experiences on the rapid.

3 How you feel – you very quickly get a feeling about the rapid which tells you if you want to run it or not.

Having considered the difficulty of the paddling, the hazards on the way, and the consequences of a mistake, you must make up your mind – paddling or carrying around. Not paddling a rapid which you feel you can not handle is a sign of good judgement and it is an essential quality in a good white-water paddler. It is often the choice which requires the most courage. If your decision is to run the rapid, then you must set about memorizing the route through it and devising your tactics. Watch yourself paddling it in your mind's eye and know when to cross, when to accelerate, how to line up for the drops. The next stage is to commit yourself. It is not the time to dwell on doubt.

Running rapids without inspecting them from the bank is a risky business. It is called 'on-sight pad-dling', and it is usually taken on by kayakers who have knowledge of the river's grading through a guide book or by word of mouth and who consider the degree of difficulty well within their capabilities.

The International River Grading System splits white water into six broad categories:

Grade I
Not Difficult
The water is flowing but there are only small shallow banks which may contains the odd boulder.

Grade II
Moderately Difficult
The way down the river is clear but simple obstructions exist. Small stoppers and small drops can be present. There are places where the current accelerates.

Grade III
Difficult
There is a route to be taken but it is recognizable from the kayak. Waves can be high and irregular. Boulders and obstructions can be numerous. Stoppers and small eddies exist.

Grade IV
Very Difficult
The route is not always clear. At this level, most paddlers choose to inspect from the bank beforehand. Rapids are continuous and the water can be heavy. Stoppers are powerful. The paddler is required to manoeuvre continually.

Grade V
Extremely Difficult
Inspection is mostly essential because serious dangers exist in the rapid. The paddling can include large drops, narrow passages, very complex boulder fields and difficult holes. Difficulties are continuous.

Grade VI
The Official Upper Limit
Water level is critical to permit paddling. The consequences of a mistake are extremely serious. May contain any white-water problems with difficult and complicated approaches.

Rivers are generally split into sections of consistent grades although it is often useful to give a grade to a specific rapid which exceeds the level of the section within which it is contained. German paddlers show the specific rapid with an index figure. So a section given II_4 is Grade II with a rapid or fall of 4. Half grades are often used for water which falls between two grades. This is indicated with a + sign after the grade: for example, III+; or by using both grades; for example, III-IV. A section of river is graded for its most commonly paddled level. This is important to know because a river section in higher conditions can be much more difficult. Some rivers, however, become easier.

The International Grading System is controversial. Some paddlers believe that rivers are too diverse in

their characteristics, degrees of difficulty, and danger levels to fit into a simple I to VI system. Others, feel that giving more information in a grade would encourage poor decision-making by paddlers who might choose to run a section entirely on the basis of its grading and not on what they see for themselves on the day. It seems likely, however, that a seventh grade will be added to the top end of the scale. This symbolizes the rise in standards and aspirations of the modern white-water paddler.

Below left: This is Grade 1 water on the River Durance in southern France.

Below: Grade 3 water.

Top right: Pulling into an eddy on Grade 3 water in the French Alps.

Right: Grade 4. Viewed from the water, the route is not clear but inspection from the bank reveals definite channels around obstructions. The paddler has a choice of lines, one along the left bank and the other on the inside of the bend.

Bottom right: Grade 5. This rapid needs to be inspected because it contains several nasty holes. To reach the exit of the rapid, the paddler must cross from the right to the left bank – quickly!

OTHER RIVER HAZARDS

Trees

Trees which have been carried along by a river in spate and then lodged on the bed leaving the current flowing through the branches are serious hazards to kayakers. This kind of problem is called a *strainer*, for obvious reasons. A paddler tangled in this kind of mess is in serious difficulties. The secret is to be conscious of the problem and give the hazard a wide berth either by walking around it or by keeping clear of it.

Trees which have fallen, or have just started to lean, often block the outsides of bends. On narrow alpine rivers in Europe, the banks are lined with coniferous forests. The weak root systems in the shallow soil frequently give way, leaving the whole river blocked off. The dense branches along the trunk form a terrible strainer.

Bends

Most of the water in a river will flow in a straight line until it hits some-thing which changes its direction This is precisely what happens to a piece of water on a bend. It continues to flow until it hits the outside of the bend which it is deflected around. This forms a deep, fast channel. The fast current keeps the deep channel scoured and, if the river bank is earth, it will erode that as well. This causes trees to topple into the water or can expose root systems which become strainers at higher water levels.

If the bank is rocky and steep, a *cushion wave* will form where the water initially hits it. The kayaker treats this wave in exactly the same way as a *cushion wave* on a boulder.

Right: A large cushion wave is formed against a rock on the outside of a bend. This piece of white water is the Jugbuster Rapid on the River Bio Bio, Chile in South America.

Below: Fallen trees creating a blockage on the River Onde in France.

BANK SCOURING

The water on a bend is fastest on the outside. It creates a deep channel by scouring the bed.

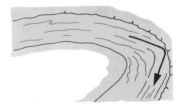

Soft, tree-lined banks are also scoured, exposing root systems and causing the tree to tilt.

CUSHION WAVE

Solid rock or artificial banks can give a spiralling cushion wave along the outside.

Spate conditions

Rivers swollen greatly by flood water or by sudden snow melt must be treated with great care. So massive is the surge of water that the kayaker often finds no hiding place. Eddies are blown out and those which exist are buried deep among the trees which once lined the banks. Only huge holes and waves remain. Bridges, which in normal times represent security and contact with the outside world, can become major hazards leaving no room for the paddler to pass underneath or trapping floating logs in its arches. For the paddler who takes a swim, a swollen river offers little help. Along its banks are helical currents set up by friction between water and land. These channel any floating objects, including swimmers into the main current making escape to the bank extremely difficult. Any river in these conditions is unrecognizable, even to local kayakers, and the safe thing to do is keep off the water

HELICAL CURRENTS

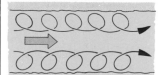

In spate conditions, helical currents, which are not always visible, form along the banks and push floating objects into the flow.

A CHOICE OF WHITE WATER

The white-water rivers of the world fall between two extremes; the wide, deep waterways which form the main arteries for carrying massive quantities of water across the earth's surface and the mountain torrents which start steep and narrow high on the hillsides. Part of the fun of running rivers is in the different experiences you get from these varied kinds of water.

Paddling on a mature, wide river can best be described as 'powerful'. The high volume of water tumbling and swirling away from the mountains creates waves and eddies on a grand scale. The stand-ing waves tower over your head as you tumble into the troughs, and the eddies boil and surge with the colossal energy of the river. The eddy lines become a wide no-man's land of swirls and currents which are difficult to paddle in. Your job as a kayaker is to avoid the largest holes by placing yourself on a good line through the rapids and surviving the crushing waves.

These rivers can usually be paddled all year around because of the massive catchment of their water supply. They are often used as a source of hydroelectric power, and the inevitable dams can create considerable fluctuations in water levels downstream.

Much of the kayaking on white water takes place on the tributaries of these great rivers or in mountainous areas where the land is not extensive enough to form them. Most of the British white-water rivers fall quickly from relatively low mountain country into less wide rivers which offer only intermittent sections of rapids. The much higher mountain country of the European Alps, with its maze of valleys, lends great distance to the steep, white-water rivers offering the paddler an enormous choice in gradient and difficulty. Because mountain rivers are so steep, water runs off quickly unless they are supplied with more. This supply comes from either snow

melt, in spring or summer, or rainfall. Glaciated areas are therefore excellent for white-water paddling because these areas are dependably seasonal.

The rivers are at their best when the weather is at its best; in the afternoon heat when the sun has warmed the mountains. Snow melt in non-glaciated regions is much less predictable and, when it occurs in early spring, it tends to come all at once. Most North American, Scandinavian, and Canadian rivers are like this.

Steep, mountainside rivers are usually shallow and very fast flowing. The paddling feels unrelenting, a continuous slalom course through boulderfields, over plunges, and into tight gullies. Eddies are small; you have to grab them quickly as they pass, and drag yourself into them to get a rest and a chance to glance downstream. Many alpine rivers of this character are barraged for hydro-electric power. This has a steadying influence on the water level downstream. Rivers without these rise and fall with the moods of the weather. Therefore, it is important to know the best level of water for paddling these rivers. Many are harder, or even impossible, in very high spate and this is where a guide book and so on are important.

Whereas in the deep, high-volume type of river, a paddler might well expect to capsize several times on the run and happily roll up, the very steep mountain rivers are a different story. Some rivers are too fast and too shallow to make attempting to roll safe and it is better to get out of the boat and on to dry land as fast as possible.

Below left: There is little water going down this stretch of river but there is still fast and furious paddling on a very steep gradient. Afon Pen-Llafar, Wales.

Below: Grade 4/5 water.

Bottom: Grade 5 water.

CHAPTER 3

BASIC KAYAK CONTROL

Your kayak is an extension of your body – more specifically, an extension of your legs and hips. Its form and shape are perfect for moving in the turbulent water of a rapid allowing you to cross the water as fast as you can run, move sideways, go backwards, roll, and even somersault. You use the kayak's shape and its interaction with the river's movements when you successfully negotiate a piece of white water. The skill of handling the boat is in knowing what the river is doing and then presenting the kayak to it so that the finished manoeuvre is the product of your work and the energy of the river. Before you can become expert in causing the boat to interact with moving water, you must first acquire good basic kayak control.

Basic kayak control includes all the elements which make up the way you create movement in your kayak with the help of the paddle. These elements are very clear when you manoeuvre on flat water where the river has little energy. To perform skilfully on white water, you must develop efficient, economic basic control on flat water. This requires you to:

● Understand the elements of basic kayak control.
● Practise and perfect them.

Your practice on flat water will also help you to build the strength and flexibility in your arms, trunk, and hips which you will need to handle rapids.

EQUIPMENT CHECK

You should develop the habit of checking your boat and equipment regularly. You are as dependent on

PADDLING FORWARDS

Above: Your hands should grip the paddle slightly wider than shoulder width.

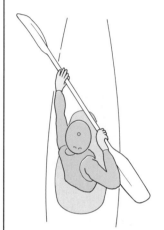

Above: Trunk rotation and arm extension form the basis of good kayak paddling technique. It is mainly a pulling exercise using trunk and arm musculature.

Above: The extension of the arm is clear here. When the blade drops into the water the paddler will draw himself/herself up to it using powerful trunk rotation.

Above: This view of the paddler through the side of the kayak shows how trunk rotation, arm extension, and the recovery of the blade are co-ordinated.

it as a pilot is on the aircraft, and you are the only engineer. Before starting to perfect your basic control you must check the following:

● Ensure that the kayak cockpit is comfortable and that the hip pads are correctly fitted.
● Check that the footrest is holding your knees comfortably in contact with the knee or thigh braces.

● Check that the paddle shaft has an ovalled grip on both sides.
● Ensure that your clothing, buoyancy aid, and spray deck do not restrict your movement.
● Check your hand position on the paddle shaft.

PADDLING FORWARDS

Once you can control the run of the kayak in a straight line, you must learn good forward-paddling technique. This is what you do most in your kayak; it helps you to cover the distance, and it is used to give you the power to get away from trouble; the 'throttle control' is here.

Paddling a kayak forwards is about locking the blade into the water and pulling yourself past it. It

BASIC KAYAK CONTROL

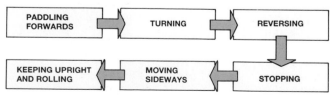

you quite naturally so long as you practise regularly. You should think of, and practise, forward paddling as a cycle of movements which fit smoothly together and not as a collection of separate parts. You will quickly learn to incorporate basic steering actions into the cycle so that the flow is not interrupted and the kayak continues to cut cleanly through the water.

Some hints for practice
• Practise accelerating to full power from gentle paddling. You should feel the pressure increase in the soles of your feet as they transmit the thrust from your trunk into the footrest. If you cannot feel this alternating pressure, then you need more trunk rotation.
• Paddle with your head relaxed but steady, and look forwards.
• Allow the paddle shaft to move away from your chest for the whole cycle.
• Exaggerate the rotation – experiment. You cannot over-rotate.

TURNING

There are two levels of turning and steering a kayak:
1 Initial turning – the sweep stroke and stern rudder.
2 Secondary turning – the low-brace turn
– the bow rudder.

The first group of strokes **initiates** turning in the kayak, while the second group is applied **once turning movement has been started.**

The sweep stroke
The forward sweep is a modified forward-paddling action; indeed, it can be incorporated into the forward-paddling cycle without causing any break in rhythm. When the kayak is still, rotate as if to start a forward-paddling stroke.
• Fully immerse the blade.
• Leave the arm extended and pull the front of the kayak away from the blade.
• Use trunk-rotation power to keep the blade in the water and the boat turning.

Paddling forwards. The left stroke finishes leaving the trunk fully rotated, and the right arm is extended for the next stroke.

is a mistake to think that the pulling action is carried out merely by the arms. It is the powerful musculature of the trunk, rather than just the small muscle which flexes the elbow, which provides the enormous propulsive force required to drive the kayak and your body-weight forwards. To engage this musculature you must concentrate on two elements of the forward paddling cycle:
• **Trunk rotation**
movement from the hips which allows each shoulder to come for-

wards as you catch water and rotate rearwards as you pass the blade. Try sawing a thick log and notice your sawing shoulder follow through with each cut. The action is very similar although you should avoid any forward and rearward jerking of the spine.
• **Arm extension**
as you rotate and reach forward to drive the blade into a new piece of water, your arm is extended fully. This gives you a long reach to the stroke and and therefore allows you to apply forward thrust over a long period.

Co-ordination
Co-ordinating trunk rotation, arm extension, and the recovery of the blade through the air will come to

FORWARD SWEEP

STERN RUDDER

EDGING AND LEANING

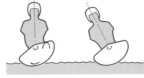

Far left: *1.* Moves the front of the boat. *2.* Gives turning and

forward thrust. *3.* Maximum turning.

Top, above, and above right: The reverse sweep. Begin with full rotation and lean slightly forward as you make the sweep.

- Keep the arm straight.
- Lift out the blade before it touches the rear of the kayak by flexing the elbow.
  You should feel:
- Your feet and knees driving the boat around in the turn.
- The grip of the fully immersed blade in the water.
- The turning effect that the straight arm gives.
- Your arm locked at the shoulder so the sweeping movement is a result of trunk rotation only.
  Imagine looking at yourself from above. Notice that the paddle shaft, your arm, and shoulder form the radius of a circle. The sweep stroke is an arc, and your spine is at the centre of the circle. The arc has three components:
  1 Is away from the bow.
  2 Is along the length of the boat.
  3 Is towards the rear.
  Each of these positions plays a part in the spin of the kayak.
- Start your forward sweep.

Above: The forward sweep is modified forward paddling.

- Say 'one' as you pull away from your feet.
- Say 'two' as you pull past your hips.
- Say 'three' as you rotate towards the rear.
  Keep the whole movement smooth, and hold the kayak level on the surface. Practise slow movements – boiling water around the paddle blade is not necessary. The boat has an optimum turning speed across the water.
  When you use a sweep stroke, you will need to see where you are going so you must practise looking forward as you rotate.

Sweep on the move
- Start the kayak moving forwards at medium speed.
- Apply the forward sweep using the one, two, three count.

- Notice what happens.
  You jump quickly between 'one' and 'two' because the water moving past takes the blade rearwards. By the time you have said 'two', the kayak has slowed and you have lots of time for number three. You can take advantage of this in your paddling. If you find that you need a lot of turning in your sweep, you emphasize that part of the arc. It could be, however, that you want to emphasize keeping the forward speed on the kayak during the sweep. You emphasize 2. If you want simply to displace the bow of the kayak then you need 1.

Reverse sweep
Exactly the same mechanical principles apply to the reverse sweep as to the forward sweep. Take care with the starting position so that you begin with full rotation towards the blade in the water. In position 3 (towards the bow), it is helpful to

LOW BRACE TURN

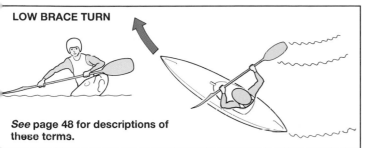

See page 48 for descriptions of these terms.

advantage of the powerful pushing action. On the river, the stern rudder is used for fine control of the boat when it is being propelled by the gradient of a wave or possibly by a powerful tail wind. Wider turning movements are made using the sweep stroke.

SECONDARY TURNING STROKES

The low brace turn

The aim of the low brace turn is to enable the kayak to turn in a long, wide arc without it losing its forward momentum. The stroke has an important function in eddy turns on the river.

● Start the kayak running.
● On the other side, set the back of the blade on the surface, level with your shoulder and away from the side of the boat.
● Lift the opposite edge using your thigh.
● Allow the kayak to continue to glide as it turns.

The function of the paddle is to give you support while you set the boat on its edge, and so it should remain flat on the water but with its

lean your trunk slightly forward as you make the sweep. This adds a little strength to what is otherwise quite a weak position.

Stern rudder

This stroke gives you sensitive steering control when the kayak is moving forwards with the minimum of interference to the speed of its run.

● Start the boat running straight – forward paddling.
● Rotate to one side and trail the rearmost blade in the water close to the kayak.
● Ensure that the blade is upright (like a rudder) and immersed.
● Push the blade gently *away* from the side of the boat. The boat turns gently to that side in response.

Now try the same position with the boat running.

● Pull the blade gently *towards* the kayak.
● The boat responds by turning a few degrees in the opposite direction. Notice that you can only make a small change of direction by this pulling action.

Practise changing sides with the stern rudder so that you can take

Below: The low brace turn has important functions in eddy turns.

leading edge raised by only a few degrees to cause the water moving towards it to pass underneath. The kayak is set on its edge to help it follow a smooth turn (called **carving**), and also because it is essential when it is applied in eddy turns on the river.

Edging and leaning

For the purpose of the low brace turn and for other white-water skills you should understand these terms clearly.

To edge a kayak, you lift one side using your knee and thigh on the brace on that side. Quite naturally, you also depress the hip and buttock on the opposite side.
- Sit on the floor with your legs in the kayak seating position.
- Raise one buttock off the floor.
You are edging! It is slightly harder when you have to lift at least half the weight of your kayak on that top thigh, of course. You have to build strength in your groin and abdomen for edging, and using a very heavy kayak is not a good way to learn.

Leaning is the term used to describe moving your upper body mass off its upright position of balance. It is the movement you make going around a corner on a bicycle. Sometimes in kayaking, you turn a corner quickly, in the

same way, and you lean to compensate as you would on a bike.

In a low brace turn, you must always edge. Whether or not you lean and to what degree depend on how tight the turn is. The stroke gives you a high degree of security on moving water, resulting in a slow, non-attacking turn. To get a faster and more aggressive turn you use a bow rudder.

The bow rudder

The bow rudder is known as a **compound stroke**. This means that it is not a single movement nor position, but rather a sequence of subtle pulls, pushes, and slices of the blade. It can function as a brake to the boat's forward speed or it can inject acceleration. It can cause a long, carving turn with no change in the kayaks' speed or it can spin the boat and shoot it off on a new course. The range of effects of the stroke is wide but fundamentals in technique are relatively simple.
- Start the boat running on still water.
- Initiate the turn using a forward sweep.
- Trunk rotate towards the turn.
- With the arm which finished the sweep, take it across the top and front of your head and hang the paddle shaft from it.

THE BOW RUDDER

The foot and knee of the outside leg drive the kayak in the turn.

The lower wrist rolls to deliver subtle changes in pressure.

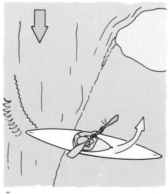

In an eddy turn, the bow rudder blade is placed into the piece of water which the paddler wishes to enter. The kayak is pivoted around it.

The bow pull control over the position of the bow and can be used on its own to steer around boulders or as an addition to a bow rudder to prolong the turn.

Left and below: The bow rudder is a sequence of pushes, pulls, and slices of the blade. In other words, the bow rudder is known as a compound stroke. It can be used either to accelerate the kayak forwards or to reduce forward speed.

It can also be used for long turns with little change in speed or rapid changes of course. Despite the versatility of the technique, fundamentally, it is very simple to execute. The diagrams below explain how it works in more detail.

- Drive the boat as far into the turn as is required.
- Finish the turn by giving a forward power stroke.

Eddy turns make the bow rudder easy because the current assists the turn. The blade is positioned with little 'opening', that is, almost parallel to the kayak side, and the finishing forward power stroke, which is in effect a short pull, is always used. It is called a **checking stroke** and prevents the kayak from sliding backwards as a result of the pendulum effect of the turn.

The bow rudder is not a stroke to be attempted half-heartedly. It needs power and commitment from the paddler to make it work. Holding back makes it impossible to achieve the wrist position and blade angle which are fundamental to the mechanics of the turn. The bow rudder uses a deep blade. It does not work with a shallow blade, and it is hard to balance if you attempt it where there is barely enough depth. It would be better to use a low brace followed by reverse sweep in these conditions.

Edging and leaning
In the eddy turn you will need a little of both. It is possible to speed up the turn by using a lot of edging. This is especially noticeable in highly rockered kayaks. White-water paddlers use this edging control if they realize half way through that a faster turn is required than they were originally intending.

The bow pull
Slicing the bow rudder blade towards your feet and out a little from the boat gives you more control over the position of the bow. This can be useful for avoiding collisions or if you want to position the bow carefully in a piece of water. The bow pull can be used on its own as a modified form of the bow rudder, or the normal position for the rudder can be sliced into the bow pull half way through the turn.

- Using the other arm, position the blade into the water, level with your knees.
- Open the leading edge of the blade so that it draws water in towards the boat.
- Drive the boat around the turn with the outside knee.

Look at the photograph and notice the following points:
- seen from the front view, the whole of the paddle shaft is on the working blade side of the boat;
- both wrists are rolled back to their full extent to 'open' the blade;
- the blade is fully immersed.
Remember:
- Always to initiate the turn with a sweep.
- That the power for the turn comes from unwinding the trunk from rotation. This is transmitted into the footrest and knee brace to drive the kayak around.

As the kayak completes the turn your wrists naturally unroll leaving the blade and lower hand in a position to drive the boat forward. Practise the whole turn on flat water.
- Aim to keep the boat moving forwards so that, as you finish, you are paddling forwards.
- Move sharply from the sweep to the bow rudder position.
- Try to feel the blade and shaft fixed in the water, like a solid post.
- Drive the kayak around it using your abdominal muscles.

Bow rudder in an eddy turn
If you want to turn out of the current into an eddy:
- Place the kayak across the eddy line using a forward sweep.
- Rotate to the turning side of the boat.
- Place the bow rudder blade into the eddy.

REVERSING

There are only a few occasions when you will actually choose to paddle your kayak in reverse but it is

---

REVERSE PADDLING

Considerable trunk rotation is used in reversing, not just to make the stroke work but also to **give you a clear view of the water behind and the exact position of the boat's rear point.** **For reverse power, drive the blade close to the edges; for steering, sweep wide.**

Powerful sideslips play an important part in controlling the kayak on moving water. The blade is buried deep to give a solid grip on the water, and the kayak is slid in towards it. This is often used as the final adjustment to the boat's position on a lead in to a rapid.

THE DRAW STROKE

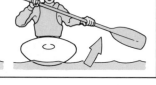

not at all uncommon to find yourself involuntarily turned in a rapid as though the kayak preferred to travel that way around. For this reason, and because some white-water techniques require you to operate in reverse, you must become skilful at paddling your boat backwards.

Firstly, you must familiarize yourself with guiding it in a straight line. The secret is not to let the boat run fast and, to check swings of the stern off course, use a good reverse sweep or two. Paddling in reverse is a pushing action, and you use even more trunk rotation than you would in going forwards. This is because the starting phase of the stroke is further to the rear than you can naturally reach. You must rotate to get the paddle into the catch phase of the stroke. The trunk unwinds as the blade is pushed past the hip. Reverse paddling is a study in trunk rotation and is good training for your forward technique.

Visibility

Seeing what lies behind you and where the stern is pointing are vital when you are working in reverse. You should take a quick glance over each shoulder, coinciding with its rotation rearwards, to fix your posi-

tion. Then it is best to sight over one shoulder. This helps you to keep the stern in sight for most of the time and prevents you from losing your datum point; this is a kind of visual balance mechanism like an artificial horizon which keeps you oriented.

Power and control

If you require a lot of power from your reversing you push the paddle deep through the water and close to the side of the kayak. If you are steering downstream and you are concerned about lining the boat up for little tongues of current, then a wide, low stroke, which is a series of reverse sweeps, is more appropriate. Practise both, so that you can select instantly the one you need.

STOPPING

Practise stopping the kayak on a fast forward run. This is quite a common action on a rapid, perhaps to avoid another paddler or to avoid meeting with something less friendly which you did not spot earlier! Stopping your kayak means arresting the momentum of the combined weight of yourself and the kayak perhaps from a speed of 12 to

15 miles an hour (20-25 km/h). That takes a lot of effort and some balance.
● Use short, jabbing, reversing strokes which keep the pressure on and reduce the turning effect.
● Using partly immersed blades helps you to reverse more quickly.
● Keep watching the obstacle.

MOVING SIDEWAYS

The paddle action which causes the kayak to sideslip across the water is called the **draw stroke**. The position of the paddle shaft is very similar to that of the bow rudder.
● Sit upright and rotate partially towards the direction to which you wish to sideslip.
● Hang the paddle shaft from the top arm reached across the top of your forehead.
● Reach away from your side with the lower arm and plant the blade into water.
● Pull yourself sideways towards the blade.
The kayak sideslips.
● Before the kayak and blade run into each other, you roll your wrist inwards and slice the blade from the water. If you need to continue the sideslip you simply repeat the draw.

water slice into shallow ground can be a wet experience.

The sculling draw

The sculling draw makes it possible to apply continuous sideslip pressure. The lower arm knifes the blade forwards and rearwards, and slight feathering of the blade on each action gives the purchase for the draw. From the sculling draw you gain continuous pressure on the sideslip. But you lose some of the power that can be applied in the conventional draw. The sculling draw requires full trunk rotation and the same raised leading edge of the kayak.

KEEPING UPRIGHT

It goes without saying that you need some kind of strategy for preventing a capsize, for kayaking on white water offers many forces which will upset your balance. The answer is the **brace**. The ability to produce a solid brace in the middle of a rapid is not just useful, it is essential.

If you are sitting on the ground and someone pushes you from the side you instinctively put out your hand flat on to the ground to regain your balance. This is exactly like a brace in a kayak, and the reflex mechanism whereby you decide instantly to do it must be transferred to your kayaking behaviour. You already know the low brace position from the turning strokes.

Without allowing your controlling hand to leave the paddle grip, you drive the back of the blade on to the water surface. The action is a pushing one, rather like a reverse paddle stroke. The purchase that you get

The draw stroke causes the boat to sideslip across the water and uses a similar paddle shaft position to that used in the bow rudder.

It is worth practising returning the blade to the draw start position by knifing it through the water after you have made the wrist roll. This is not always faster but it can be helpful for controlling the direction of the sideslip.

● If the kayak starts to swing off the course of the sideslip while you are pulling on the draw, check the swing by drawing towards the bow or stern accordingly.

Things to remember about the draw

● The top arm stays in its high position until the draw is completed.
● Your vision must not be obstructed by the top arm, and you look *under* it.
● Water should pass *under* the hull in the sideslip, not over the deck. It is necessary to raise slightly the leading edge of the kayak if you are moving powerfully in a sideslip to ensure that this happens.
● If you are doing a lot of successive **draws**, let the top hand share the work of the wrist roll. It can be quite strenuous.
● Keep looking forward but be aware of the depth. A through-the-

THE SCULLING DRAW

The paddle is feathered as it slices along the length of the kayak. This gives continuous sideslip pressure. An excellent flat-water practice, this develops the paddler's sensitivity to the blade and 'feel' for slicing.

THE HIGH BRACE

The high brace is the main part of your defences. When the river throws you around and does its best to get you off balance, you respond with a brace. The

paddle blade's grip on water is transmitted through the trunk to produce a reflexive hip rotation which straightens the kayak. A good paddler can see it coming.

from the contact of the blade with the surface lets you regain your balance. The blade will have sunk below the surface slightly because of the momentary load placed on it and you recover it by allowing your elbows to drop downwards. This rotates the blade and allows it to be knifed vertically to the surface.

The high brace

When the capsizing forces are large and you are completely overbalanced, the upright body position of the low brace makes it impractical to use. The high brace is the reflex stroke which you are most likely to need.
• Hold the paddle shaft at shoulder height with the blade driving face down on your right-hand side.
• Overbalance to that side.
• Eventually the blade hits the surface.
• Drive the kayak upright using your hips and thighs, and *pull* on the paddle shaft.
• Bring your trunk back into balance.
The secret in the brace is the action used to bring the boat upright. In this example, the right thigh lifts the edge of the kayak back to the horizontal. This is actually a powerful rotation of the pelvis transmitted into the thigh bone. The action was used before in the edging technique but this time it is applied suddenly. By using good hip action at the correct time in the high brace, you reduce dramatically the load on the blade and improve your chances of staying on the surface of the water.

Further points to remember
• Try to keep the paddle shaft below head height. Your shoulder joints can move into an unstable position from there and you risk dislocation.
• Aim to keep the paddle shaft close to horizontal. The more it departs from horizontal the less support there is in the bracing blade.
• Fight it. Do not give up without trying for a brace, and do it purposefully.
• Practise alternating high braces from one side to the other.

Above: The high brace is used when you are overbalanced by the capsizing forces.

Below: The sculling brace preserves the paddle blade support.

• Do practise. It is the only way you can get it into your body's reflex memory. Work at it.
• To recover the paddle blade after a successful high brace, roll the wrists inwards and you will knife out vertically.

Sculling brace
You can preserve the paddle blade support in a high brace by keeping it on the move with a sculling action forwards and rearwards across the surface. A slight wrist roll in each direction of scull lifts the leading edge causing it to track on the surface. Keeping the paddle shaft low and close to the horizontal is still important because, in effect, you are hanging quite a lot of your upper body weight from it.

LINKING STROKES

Although each stroke has been examined separately, it would be a mistake to think of moving a kayak around as a sequence of isolated, precise paddle positions. If you watch a skilful paddler at work, it is a single flowing action resulting in positive boat movements and no distinction in the strokes. There is, however, no doubt that he or she has mastered the basic kayak handling strokes. What you are seeing is a subtle blending of these strokes often superimposed one upon the other. This kind of expertise comes from hard practice, a feel for the boat in water, and an understanding of how the stokes work. It is always a delight to watch a skilful paddler.

Below: The sculling brace. The kayak is held in the stopper, and the paddler steadies himself.

Ways to improve stroke linking

• Practise connecting strokes by setting a flat water course involving tight and wide turns, reversing, moving sideways, and even bracing.
• Rehearse specific stroke links, such as repeated draw strokes: forward paddling stroke into reverse sweep; bow rudder to forward paddling.
• Perfect *slicing*, and experiment with it. Slicing occurs when you knife the blade either through the water or across the surface to take it into its new starting position. It is a fast way to connect strokes on the same side, and you can often use the brief slice phase to help maintain control of the boat.

Other examples of slicing include: high brace surface slide to forward power stroke; forward paddle stroke slice to draw; forward paddle stroke slice out to position 3 of forward sweep.

THE ESKIMO ROLL

You can be certain that you will capsize often in white water. Sometimes, it will be deliberate because you can not resist standing your boat on its end in a beautiful wave. At other times, it will be because of a mistake you made in a line or in anticipating a current. And sometimes it will happen for reasons you are unable to fathom. So now you are upside down and, for a few moments at least, you do not need to think about paddling the rapids.

Now you need the Eskimo Roll. A voice in your head says get out and grab some cheap air. The canoeist inside you takes over and you stay put, ready to roll.

THE ESKIMO ROLL

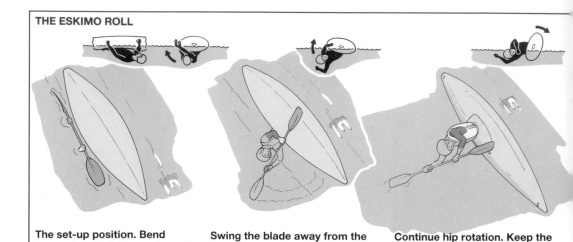

The set-up position. Bend forwards and sideways towards the surface. Paddle blades and shaft are in the air.

Swing the blade away from the boat's side. Now apply hip rotation and impart it to the thighs.

Continue hip rotation. Keep the head low, and the body in the water until the last possible moment.

• Lean forward, nose towards the foredeck.

• Pull the paddles from wherever they are to align them alongside the kayak.

• Push them out into the air, clear above the water surface.

• With the forward arm, take the paddle shaft away from the side of the boat to a 90-degree position.

• With the same hip movement that you used in the high brace, drive the boat upright on the paddle side.

• The kayak pops upright and your body follows mysteriously.

• You instinctively grab a lungful of air, a quick snort drains your nose, and you are ready for more of the same kind of action.

A closer look at the roll

Learn to roll your kayak, preferably under the guidance of another paddler with instructional experience. The movements are not difficult; there are many variations of learning progressions for you to try. You must be patient, however, because your internal learning system takes its own time to sort out the sequence of movements. Many people learn after only a small number of attempts. Others naturally take longer but I have never seen anyone, who has continued to try, fail to get there.

Water confidence

If you are not reasonably relaxed hanging upside down in your kayak in the calm clear water of a training pool, the priority is to familiarize yourself with the position.

• Have someone stand by while you play around under water.

• Try picking something off the bottom and change it to the other hand on the surface across the upturned hull.

• Lean forward (nose on front deck), wrap your arms around the boat, and let your partner roll you up.

• Hang upside down – stretch your head towards the surface and swim the kayak to the side. Let your partner pull you up again when you have had enough.

Equipment

While you are beginning to learn the stages of the roll, it is best to wear only the minimum of clothing and no buoyancy aid or helmet. Also, to make the job easier, wear a nose-clip if the water is hurting the lining of your nose. A pair of goggles or a diver's face mask would be extremely helpful aids for the familiarization drills above and for rolling training.

The hip movement

The key to the mystery of kayak roll-ing lies here. Understand the hip movement, learn to feel it working, and rolling the kayak will be light, effortless work.

• Lie on your back on the floor.

• Rotate your hips so that your legs lie one on top of the other.

• Try again, making it a single, sudden action.

• Now imagine you are in your kayak, knees in the braces, and lying back.

• Try the movement.

For the moment, think only about this twisting movement which is causing the boat to rotate.

Now get on the water and grip on to something solid, such as the pool side or a paddle shaft held by your partner, at the level of your hip.

• Lower your near shoulder into the water and pull the boat with you.

• Pause.

• Use the sudden hip movement you have practised to right the kayak.

• Your body follows it.

• Try again – lie back as you apply the hip movement.

• Again. This time lower your trunk fully into the water and capsize the kayak completely.

You should feel:

• A stretching of the sides of your trunk, especially above the hips.

• The very first movement after the pause in the water is the rotation of

Keep the blade in the water until you have got a breath, and have oriented yourself. Continue paddling.

Above: Start from a half-capsize position. Drive the kayak upright with a powerful hip rotation and knee lift. When the movement

Right: Practising rolls by placing your head into your partner's cupped hands trains you in several important aspects: 1. Stretching towards the surface before the hip movement. 2. Keeping your head and shoulders low while applying hip movement.

'clicks' with you, work from a complete capsize. When you get better, try it with one hand: then one finger.

the hips and lifting of the kayak with the thigh.
- No strain on your arms because your body naturally *follows* the boat's rotation.
- A fast movement.
- That your lower body is moving independently of your upper body.
    Try the following action.
- Capsize away from your partner who is holding the paddle shaft.
- Look for your partner (underwater).
- Reach for the paddle shaft and make your hands comfortable.
- Apply the hip movement.
    Finally, your partner stands with cupped hands about 30 centimetres (1 foot) below the surface.
- Capsize.
- Place your head in your partner's hands.
- Apply hip movement.
- Keep lying back.
The aim of this exercise is to keep your head in the water as you rotate the kayak upright.

Using the paddle

If your hip movement is working you could probably roll with anything in your hands to give a little purchase – a swim float, broken paddle blade, your partner's wetsuit boots! It is, of course, perfectly feasible to roll using your empty hands paddling on the surface!

Using your paddle:
- Try some high braces, allowing yourself to recover from a position where all of your trunk is in the water.
- Remember, when the blade touches the water, apply hip movement. Leave your body in the water.
    Now let your partner support the blade end in the water.
- Fall over into a capsize.
- Apply hip movement and lie back.

The starting position

Practise this position.
- The body is forward.
- The front arm is reaching forward.
- The paddle shaft is alongside the kayak.
    This is how you will begin your roll. It is the position you move to whenever you capsize, regardless of where your paddles or body may have been. It is an easy position to recall when you are disoriented by a sudden capsize, and it cues in your memory for the rolling movement. In shallow water, it protects your face and it ensures that you capsize into a stable position rather than floating awkwardly at an angle.
    Capsize and go into this position.
- Stretch towards the surface and push the whole paddle shaft well into the air.

- Swing the front blade round to a 90-degree angle, following it with your trunk.
- Apply your old friend – *hip movement.*
- Continue to pull the paddle rearwards.
- *You are up.*

If you have difficulties

- Use the mask or goggles to check the paddle positions, for example, above the surface and round to 90 degrees.
- Ask someone to watch for your hip movement.
- Timing is important. Do not use hip movement before the paddle is in the 90-degree position.

Final tips

- Take plenty of rests when you are learning.
- Try to watch others learning.
- Watch good rollers in the pool.
- The lie-back in the rolling makes the management of your body weight much easier. Once you can roll well, you will be able to work without it.
- Practise your successful roll in cold water and then in white water.
- If you are having a lot of failures, increase the paddle leverage by moving your back hand on to the blade and front hand further down the shaft.

CHAPTER 4

BASIC WHITE-WATER TECHNIQUE

The manoeuvres which you must be able to carry out to run a piece of white water are simply to be able to enter and exit from the current and to cross it. When you climb into your kayak at the river bank, you are out of the influence of the main current. Either you will be in an eddy of slack water or you will be in the much slower-moving water close to the bank. The kayak will be pointing upstream. Entering the current from this position is called **breaking in**. Pulling out of the current into an eddy or slacker water at the bank is called **breaking out**. Collectively, these two manoeuvres are called **eddy turns** because they make use of the eddy and its proximity to the current to turn the kayak. The paddler's job is to get the water to do the work so that he or she can concentrate on saving energy and enjoying the action.

Good eddy turns are composed of three elements:
● Balance – dealing with the forces of the turn so that you remain stable in the boat through the correct use of edging.
● Accuracy – positioning the kayak in such a way as to be sure to make the turn and to use the energy of the water to your greatest advantage.

● Timing – using paddle strokes positively, economically, and in a suitable order.

THE BREAK-IN

Firstly, decide where the eddy line is. It is your most important reference point. Now make a break-in to the current on your right.
● Accelerate across the eddy, aiming to hit the eddy line at an angle of about 45 degrees.
● Drive the kayak across the eddy line using a forward sweep on your left.
● Watch the nose of the boat. As it hits the eddy line, lift the upstream edge (left).
● Use a low brace turn on the right.
● The kayak slides forwards and turns downstream.
● Level off and paddle forward.
It is important that the kayak continues to move forwards throughout the turn so that you cross the eddy line completely with the whole kayak. Edging the kayak does two things:
1 It keeps the upstream edge out of the descending water which would dearly love to press on it and cause an upstream capsize.
2 It allows the current to grip the

lower edge, helping to pull the boat around in the turn.

Stroke timing
Powerful forward strokes are needed to begin the boat accelerating in the eddy. In the sweep, emphasize the middle third of the stroke and you will find that you have started the edging *before* this stroke is finished. The low brace turn provides you with a good solid handrail to use as you keep the edging on through the turn. Remember to keep your elbows high, lean slightly, and edge.

A more powerful turn
If you require the boat to accelerate throughout the turn, you replace the low brace turn with a bow rudder. The bow rudder blade is driven deeply into the current water immediately after the sweep. Both edging and lean are required, and you balance the swing of the turn against the grip of the blade in the water. This is tippy, but very fast!

THE BREAK-OUT

The three phases of a break-out are:
● The line-up – spot the eddy and move towards it well in advance.

Left and below: The break-in using a low brace turn. Level off and paddle forwards. Note that the boat should continue to move forwards throughout the turn so that you are able to cross the eddy line completely with the whole kayak.

THE BREAK-IN

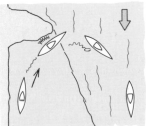

Start from an eddy and drive into the current by crossing the eddy line and turning downstream. Raise the upstream edge.

THE BREAK OUT

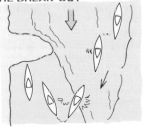

Move towards the eddy well in advance. Push the boat across the eddy line. Raise the outside edge as the kayak goes into the turn.

- Angle of approach – set the angle at which to cross the eddy line.
- The turn – use a stroke sequence to suit the speed of the turn and depth of penetration into the eddy.

If you make a mistake with a break-out, the result is usually to be swept past the eddy. This is no fun if you needed to get out at that eddy.

How it feels

- Know the eddy is coming up and watch for it.
- Decide to take it. If you do not like it move on, but do **decide**.
- Start moving towards it immediately by:
Pointing and sprinting for it.
Or using draw strokes and forward paddling.
Or reverse ferry gliding.
- Pass close to the obstruction forming the eddy.
Drive the kayak across the eddy line using a forward sweep.
- Apply edging as you cross the eddy line.
- Use a low brace turn to complete the manoeuvre.
- Forward checking stroke. Boat level.

A **bow rudder** in the eddy instead of the low brace gives you a greater degree of control once you cross

---

the eddy line but it is not quite as stable for slightly nervous paddlers.

Whatever choice of strokes you make, you must attack the break-out with determination. It takes strength and aggression, as well as technique, to pull out of the grip of the current.

THE S-TURN

The S-turn is a consecutive break-in and break-out. It is one way to cross a tongue.

Setting the eddy line target

Some eddies are huge, extending for 100 metres (over 300 feet) or so downstream; others are small and narrow – perhaps not even as long as your kayak. Both offer the opportunity to break out but the second is easy to miss. In the first case, it does not matter very much where you cut the eddy line provided you do cut it. In the second, you must cut it close to the source of the eddy. When you first spot your eddy line, make an imaginary mark on it to aim for. This mark is the **eddy line target** and it helps you with the accuracy of your boat placement. Experiment with eddy line targets, on the same eddy line and in different eddy shapes.

Left and below: The break-out using a bow rudder. Using this stroke gives you a greater degree of control as soon as you have crossed the eddy line but, if you are apprehensive, it may be better to use the low brace turn which is rather more stable than the bow rudder.

Sometimes setting the target too close to the source leaves you with no room to make the turn. If you set the target too far down the eddy, it might reduce the current differential so much that you fail to make the eddy.

Angle and speed of approach

Given a wide, well-defined eddy, cross the eddy line at about 45 degrees. This angle becomes important when we look at more difficult eddy forms, such as a long, thin eddy in the mid-stream. This time a wide angle of approach is needed to prevent overshooting and re-entering the current.
● Line up by passing a little wide of the eddy source.
● Set a wide angle of approach so you do not overshoot.
● Power the kayak forwards and across the eddy line with a strong forward sweep.
● Stab the bow rudder blade into the eddy water and pull the kayak into it.
● Hard checking stroke.

Consider an eddy where the current is moving quickly away from the eddy line. In this case, the paddler's line requires a very narrow angle of approach or he or she will be carried

THE S-TURN

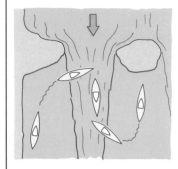

This is one way to get to an eddy across a tongue. Break in moving flat-out, aim for the new eddy line, and break out.

THE EDDY LINE TARGET

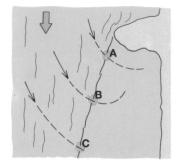

Set your target correctly. B is the best. A leaves no room to turn the kayak. At C the eddy line is indistinct.

away from the eddy, further downstream.
● Line up using draw strokes.
● Skirt close to the source of the eddy, maintaining a narrow angle of approach. Keep the boat moving slowly, by reversing if necessary.
● Displace the bow of the kayak into the eddy using a forward sweep.
● Rotate quickly to catch the eddy water with the bow rudder blade.
● Checking stroke.

Reverse eddy turns

Practising eddy turns while reversing is excellent training for boat **balance**, but it is also important to be able to handle them for the time when you accidentally get turned in a rapid and have to use a break-out to face downstream again. Firstly, look at the stroke which you use to steady yourself through the eddy turn. It is called the **reverse brace**. It is essentially a high brace with the following modifications:

ANGLE OF APPROACH

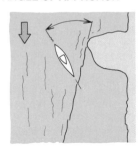

The angle at which you cross the eddy line is called the angle of approach. Take it into account when lining up for an eddy. It is important when you tackle more difficult eddy forms.

USING A WIDE ANGLE

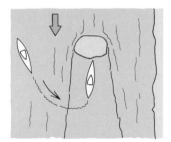

Long, narrow eddies are common at steep banks and behind boulders. Set a wide angle of approach so that you do not overshoot the narrow strip of slack water.

USING A NARROW ANGLE

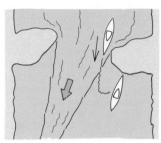

Sideslip close in towards the eddy line. Tuck the nose in behind the boulder using sector 1 of a sweep. Reach quickly for a bow rudder deep in the eddy water.

- The blade is held slightly in front of the body line.
- Because the kayak is moving in reverse, the leading edge of the trailing blade is slightly raised. The kayak is edged towards the trailing blade.

The reverse break-in
- Line up the boat in the eddy to strike the eddy line at an angle of 45 degrees.
- Accelerate towards the eddy line

using reverse power strokes.
- Raise the upstream edge as the stern approaches the eddy line.
- Reverse sweep to drive the stern into the current.
- Reverse brace on the downstream side.
- Slice to reverse paddling and level off.

It is a great help to balance if you look over your downstream shoulder throughout the whole of this manoeuvre.

The reverse break-out
- Spot the eddy; set the target.
- Line up using drawstrokes and reverse paddling.
- Watch the eddy over your upstream shoulder.
- Drive the stern across the eddy line using reverse sweep.
- Start edging (raise outside edge).
- Reverse brace.
- Check with reverse power stroke.

Once again, the paddler looks

Left: The S-turn break-in is followed by the break-out.

Below: Let the boat turn downstream.

Right: The use of the bow rudder in an eddy.

REVERSE BREAK-IN

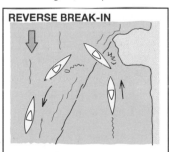

REVERSE BREAK-OUT

over the shoulder on the reverse brace side for the whole of the manoeuvre.

Eddy line spin

Once again, this manoeuvre has a great value purely as a training exercise – this time for *accuracy* of boat placement, as well as *balance*. Start by sitting in the eddy close to the eddy line.

• Push the front half of the kayak across the eddy with forward sweep.

• Edge only slightly downstream.

• Hold the boat from slipping into the current with a short reverse sweep.

• The kayak spins.

• Use a forward sweep in the current to spin the bow into the eddy.

• Reach into the eddy with bow rudder and pull in. The kayak slips downstream naturally as the spin is made.

You can make the spins continue for as long as you have an eddy line, and it is perfectly feasible to start reversing into the current and reversing out. The eddy line spin is used as a means of getting a boat turned from reverse to facing forwards in a rapid where the paddler does not wish to enter the eddy but wants to continue in the current. In this case the paddler uses only half

of the spin as shown in the illustration (positions 1 and 2), and then pulls out into the current. Notice that in the continuous eddy line spin, the sweeps alternate from forward to reverse. A skilful paddler can place the blade of the sweep (forward and reverse) *in the current* each time. With this kind of touch, the blade barely moves while the boat drives on in continuous rotation.

The transfer of edging throughout the spins is very subtle indeed. In a powerful eddy line, where the water is boiling and swirling, it is a very skilful paddler who will attempt eddy line spins.

Crossing the current

The simplest and most controlled way to cross a current is the **ferry glide**. In the forward ferry glide, the kayak faces upstream.

Imagine you are sitting at the edge of an even-flowing current.

• Push out into the current and hold your position by paddling forwards.

• Direct the nose of the kayak from straight into the current to pointing slightly towards the opposite bank.

• You feel the current pushing on the front of the boat.

• You continue to paddle forwards and the boat glides sideways across the current.

Practise first where the traverse of the river will take you across an even flow. If the kayak suddenly swings broadside to the current, you regain the angle using one or two good sweep strokes.

Setting the angle

Do not try to set the angle of the boat to the current until you are completely into the flow. You can get away from the bank or from an eddy by drawing into the current or by paddling quickly forwards with only the slightest angle to the flow and then drifting on to your ferry glide line. To increase the speed of your ferry glide traverse, set a wider angle to the current and paddle faster. If you feel that you are losing control bring the bow back towards the current.

Crossing uneven current

When the piece of river you are traversing has jets of faster water superimposed on the main current the same ferry glide rules apply.

• Push off and set the angle and paddling speed.

• When you hit the faster water, reduce the angle and maintain your paddling speed.

• When you regain the slower water increase the angle.

When you move on to the faster

THE EDDY LINE SPIN

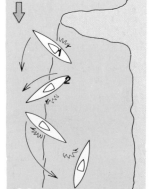

Above: Start at the head of the eddy line. Edge and push half the kayak into the current. Hold it across the line, helping the spins with forward/reverse sweeps.

FORWARD FERRY GLIDE

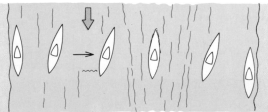

Above: Draw away from the bank. Set the angle to the current. Paddle forwards to hold

ground and as the boat crosses, respond to changes in flow speed by altering the angle.

THE ANGLE OF THE FERRY GLIDE

Right: If you widen the angle of the ferry glide, you have to paddle faster to cross quicker. If the current is fast, use a narrow angle to keep your speed in control.

water, you will momentarily need to lift the upstream edge until the whole boat is in the new current. You can then level off.

Reverse ferry glide

Mastery of the reverse ferry glide is essential for the white-water paddler, especially when he or she is paddling a rapid 'on sight', that is, without the advantage of inspection from the bank. The same principles of boat speed and angle apply as for the forward ferry glide. Again, choose an even, uninterrupted traverse line to start with.

• Draw into the current.
• Set a narrow angle and look around over your downstream shoulder.
• Use wide reverse paddling strokes to help control the angle.
• You keep looking over the downstream shoulder as you make the traverse.

If you lose the angle completely and the boat swings broadside, use forward and reverse sweeps to swing the stern back into the flow. Again, practise manoeuvring in uneven current and also try changing direction of your traverse in midstream.

Some final points on ferry glides

• Read the current well before you set off.
• Be determined to take control of the boat.
• Get to know the boat angle by 'feel'.
• Be aware of your position with respect to the river bed as you traverse; it is easy to lose ground downstream.
• Watch for boulders which might interfere with the traverse.
• Develop flexibility of the trunk of your body.

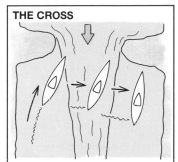

THE CROSS

To move across a tongue between two eddies, enter the current at speed and let a fast ferry glide do the work.

THE CROSS

If two eddies are separated by a narrow jet of very fast water, the paddler moves from one to the other using a cross. It is simply a very fast ferry glide.
• Drop back in the eddy to give yourself room to accelerate.
• Power the kayak across the eddy aiming to cross the eddy line at a narrow angle.
• As the nose of the kayak reaches the eddy line lift the upstream edge.
• Shoot across the narrow jet keeping the upstream edge raised.
• Use a forward power stroke on the downstream edge.
• As the kayak enters the new eddy quickly change the edging to the other side.
The cross is completed.

If the kayak starts to lose momentum in the middle of the jet, use a forward power stroke or two on the downstream side to keep the speed of the boat on.

Top left, bottom left, and above: The cross is used to move between two eddies separated by a narrow jet of fast water.

61

CROSSING ON A WAVE

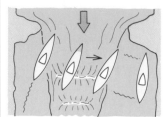

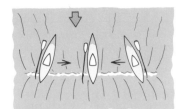

If there is a wave, however small, in the tongue, use it. Surf the kayak on the upstream side of the wave angling it to the flow.

Trail a stern rudder as you cross the wave to help steer the boat and keep it on the wave. The blade will go on the upstream side and this edge is raised.

A change of direction on a wave cross. Roll the boat on to its other edge. Push away with the stern rudder to turn. Change sides to an upstream rudder.

Crossing on a wave

Using the ramp on the face of a standing wave is a very neat and effortless way to make a cross.
● Drive the nose of the kayak out of the eddy into the trough upstream of a green wave.
● Use a narrow ferry glide angle as for the normal cross.
● Raise the upstream edge.
The kayak runs smoothly across the wave face delivering you into the eddy on the opposite side.
● Change edges as you enter the new eddy.
A paddler should always look for a wave if he or she wants to cross a current. Even the tiniest of dips in the water surface will help to shoot the boat on its way. Getting the angle to the current right is essential although it is possible to play around with it once you are established on the wave face.
Pick a long green wave.
● Drop the boat on to the wave face with a little forward speed.
● Keep the upstream edge raised.
● As the kayak loses speed on the cross and looks like pulling off the wave, trail a stern rudder on the upstream side.
● Guide the bow back into the trough.
● Hold the stern rudder in place.
The cross continues quite happily.
Stern ruddering on the upstream side while keeping the upstream edge raised takes a little practice but works superbly well. The trailing blade is working like the fin on a surfboard, while the kayak runs on its downstream rail. On a good

wave, you can change the direction of the cross:
● Push away with the arm controlling the trailing blade.
● The kayak turns square on to the wave.
● Change to lifting the opposite edge.
● Transfer the stern rudder to the new side.
● Continue the cross in the new direction.

The S-cross

It might be that the wave between the two eddies is not a clean, green wave but is rather a haystack, pointed and frothing on its peak. The absence of length and the steeper face on this wave make the conventional wave cross impracticable because the kayak would run down the steep wave face and bury itself in the trough. This causes it to stand on end and shoot out of the wave skywards. Fun, but not what

was intended, so an S-cross is needed.
● Face the boat to cut the eddy line at a wide angle.
● Accelerate across the eddy line to turn the boat downstream.
● Aim to hit the wave so that your seat passes over its crest.
● Brace on the crest.
● The kayak shoots down the wave into the eddy.
● Change edging as you hit the new eddy.
This is very much a manoeuvre to be made mostly by feel because there is little chance to see around you in the middle of the haystack. Shooting fast and blind off the haystack into the eddy is challenging stuff, and you must be quick to transfer the edging when you feel the boat hit the eddy. It is useful to think your way through the whole move several times, rehearsing the brace and edging as you make the imaginary cross.

THE S-CROSS

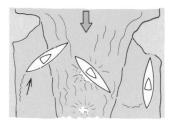

Let the kayak run on to the top of the pointed wave in the tongue. Raise the upstream edge. Power off the wave into the eddy.

Left: Crossing on a wave using a stern rudder. You will need to practice this technique but, once you have mastered it, it works very well.

Right: 'The Vacuum Cleaner' in Corsica is one of Europe's best-known stoppers. Here it is complete with a paddler and a high-volume kayak.

Below: Always enter stoppers under full power and keep the power on while you are in there.

DEALING WITH STOPPERS

'The Washing Machine', 'The Bacon Slicer', 'The Vacuum Cleaner' are the names of three illustrious stoppers on rivers in Europe. Like many others well known to paddlers on rivers all around the world, they are focal points, major challenges on sections of rivers. Pitting your skill and strength against those infamous monsters is exactly what the spirit of white-water paddling is all about. Unknown stoppers on seldom-paddled sections of rivers need to be treated with great caution, especially where they are formed on artificial structures, such as weirs and sluices.

Paddling through stoppers

If you find yourself on course for a large stopper or, if you have decided that you want to run one deliberately, the tactics are simple.

• Accelerate from about two or three boat lengths away.

• Keep the speed on as you run down into the slot.

• As the foaming wave rolls up the deck and hits you on the chest, reach over it and stab it deep in the back with your blade.

- If it is a surface stopper you will be able to feel the downstream current pulling the blade forwards. Use this to keep pressure on to drive the boat forwards.

Some stoppers give the boat a twist and try to slow it sideways as if trying to get a better grip. If you feel this happening, hold the kayak square to the stopper by digging deep with alternate blades. Keep pointing downstream.

Side surfing

Find a small surface stopper which you know is safe and which has a good, deep run out downstream. Now you are going to deliver yourself into its teeth. Let it have you sideways!
- Cross into the slot of the stopper from the side.
- Lift the upstream edge and set a high brace on to the foaming wave on your downstream side.
- The kayak is bouncing in the slot. Water is hissing under the hull.

- Now try to take some weight off the brace.
- Sit up and try sculling the blade rearwards a little.
- Quickly turn the blade over and scull forwards on a *low brace* – elbows up.
- Scull back on a high brace.
- Try to take your weight on your buttocks, not on the paddle shaft.

Now for getting out.
- Change your high brace into a forward paddling stroke by slicing in forwards and partially wrist rolling it into a half brace, half driving blade.
- A few strokes and the kayak shoots out the end of the stopper and off downstream.

The purpose of the side-surfing exercise is threefold:
1 It is challenging and excellent fun.
2 You could land in this position accidentally on a more serious rapid.
3 It teaches you how to escape from the stopper.

Above: Side surfing in the stopper slot. Apart from being good fun, this exercise teaches you how to escape from a stopper if you land in one accidentally on a serious rapid.

Here are some points to remember about side surfing.
- High-volume kayaks with broad, rounded sides and buoyant ends are much more forgiving than low-volume kayaks.
- If the circulating wave is high you must use a high brace.
- If it is very small try a low brace.
- In medium-sized waves alternating between both works well.
- Your aim is to place as little weight as possible on the brace. This prevents you from exhausting yourself and thereby cutting off your escape.
- Beware of letting the paddle shaft get above your head. In this position, the paddle shaft can move

Top: High bracing in a stopper. A high brace must be used if the circulating wave is high.

Above: The paddler is climbing out of the stopper slot stern first.

rearwards with the brace and it takes relatively little force to dislocate the shoulder.

● When you get held in a side surf, try to spend a few moments to 'rest' and work out a plan for the exit.

There are three possible ways out:

1 Out of the end (as shown).
2 Capsize and roll.
3 Skyrocket.

The capsize in a surface stopper uses the drag of your body to pull the kayak through the wave. The exit is not instantaneous after the capsize.

● Take the brace away and take a good deep breath.
● Tuck forward as for a roll and

EXITING

Exiting from the end of a stopper. Paddle and brace to the end. Push the nose into the flow.

EXIT AND SKYROCKET

Escaping can be by combining the end exit with the skyrocket.

SKYROCKETING

The pressure of flow on the sunken rear end squirts the boat out.

CAPSIZE AND ROLL-OUT

Capsizing can create enough drag to take you clear.

overbalance downstream.
- Hold the paddles against the sides of the kayak.
- Wait and listen for the turbulence to subside.
- When it does, paddles in position and roll up.

It is possible to open out after the capsize and even hold the paddles above your head to create more drag. This works but you need good, deep water downstream of the wave. The tuck works well and keeps you and your bits secure!

The skyrocket is merely an adaptation of the out-of-the-end exit. The ends of the stopper slot often slope steeply upwards to the platform of water at normal river level.
- Drive the kayak forward to the stopper end. Using the scull and slice to forward power which was discussed earlier.
- Push the nose of the boat deep into the downstream moving water.
- As the bow pulls around downstream, let the stern swing deeply into the stopper slot.
- Try to help the swing with sweep strokes but do not overdo it or you will surf in the other direction.
- Keep the kayak square and it will be squirted out of the stopper wave. Sometimes this results in a back ender leaving you capsized. Again you wait until the turbulence eases and then roll up.

The next thing to practise, of course, is exiting from the end of the stopper which is behind you.
- Scull the high brace blade rearwards.
- Roll your wrist so that you use a wide reverse power stroke to drive the boat backwards.
- Keep repeating this until you penetrate the downstream current. The reverse skyrocket is clearly very similar to the forward version.

Finally, here is a system which takes you out of a stopper which has a very deep slot and whose length is not much more than the kayak.
- In front of the nose and beyond the rear of the kayak lie two ramps.
- Run the boat up any one of these gradients and then let it fall back into the slot.
- Use the momentum from that to take you up the opposite ramp.
- Run the boat backwards and forwards across the slot until you have enough momentum to get up one of the gradients and clear of the stopper.

Deep-circulating stoppers

Do not attempt to side surf deep stoppers. Even if the back tow looks short, they are extremely difficult, and frequently impossible, to stay upright in. The kayak is drawn into the slot which is directly below the vertically falling water. It is almost impossible to prevent the water from landing on the deck, and its great weight cannot be resisted by the paddler. A capsize is inevitable and rolling merely takes you back to the same position. Swimming out and/or rescue is your only hope of escape.

It is best to steer clear of vertical weirs, sluices, and low-head dams. If, however, you are faced with such an obstacle and it is too late to do anything else but paddle over it the plan is:
- Accelerate as hard as you can and keep the pressure on.
- Aim to clear the lip of the drop like a jet leaving an aircraft carrier.
- Think of becoming airborne.
- Once you are in the air, get ready for your first paddle stroke which you use as soon as the first part of the boat lands.
- Use rapid strokes to accelerate away from the weir face.
- Find out if there are any more like that on the river!

The principle here is to jump as much of the stopper's influence as possible by taking advantage of the height of the drop. It could be a desperate attempt so try to be positive and channel your fear into physical strength.

The kayak rides broadside on to the cushion wave and hits the boulder. You are held for a moment across the current.

Lift the upstream edge of the kayak well before the boulder is hit, and use the boulder to brace on. It is worth practising this manoeuvre on fast, shallow water.

BROADSIDING

Hitting things side-on in a rapid can be a common occurrence in shallow rivers and, sooner or later, every paddler finds himself or herself momentarily held across the current on an obstruction such as a boulder.
● Raise the upstream kayak edge immediately. It is even better if you can do this just before the boat makes contact.

● Use the boulder to help you with this by bracing the paddle on it, resting your elbow on it or leaning the downstream shoulder against it.
● Push or pull forwards or backwards off the obstruction maintaining the raised upstream edge. Usually one direction is easier than the other according to how the boat has lodged.

This is easy to do so long as you are quick or, preferably, in advance with the edging. You should practise this but make sure:
● That you do it in shallow water.
● That other paddlers are standing by and can *stand up* downstream of the boulder if you need help.
● That you do not pick a boulder which is undercut on its upstream

side. Fast, shallow water is ideal practice ground.

Cushion waves
● If you broadside on to a boulder which has a cushion wave on its upstream side, the same procedure applies except that you brace (high or low) on the wave in order to lift the upstream edge. If you can easily reach over the wave to the rock, then use it to brace on.

BENDS

Tight bends on narrow rivers pose the initial problem of cutting off your view downstream. It could easily be that on or after the bend there is a serious blockage. If you have

BROADSIDING ON TO A BOULDER

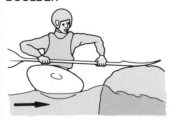

Before you touch the obstruction, raise the upstream edge and prepare for a downstream brace. If it is a small boulder, low brace on top of it. If it is a wall or a high rock, use your elbow or shoulder on it and shuffle along.

BRACING ON A CUSHION WAVE

Again, raise the upstream edge well in advance of hitting the wave. Use the rising column of water in the wave to brace on as though it were a boulder. In this position, the cushion gives a superb padded ride around the obstruction.

RUNNING A TIGHT BEND

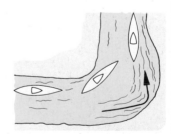

Approach the bend on its inside in the slow-moving water until you can see across to the exit. If this is clear let the boat run into the fast water leaving the bend. If you have to run the outside, raise the inside edge and trail a stern rudder on that side.

inspected the river and it is clear that the only problem lies in getting around the bend without getting caught up with trees or rock on the outside, then adopt the following procedure.

● Approach the bend from the bank that leads to the inside of the curve.

● Allow yourself to be carried on around the bend when you see that you are clear of obstructions on the outside.

● The current takes you across to the fast water leaving the bend.

If you find yourself on course for an obstruction on the outside of the bend – stop and reverse ferry glide to the inside. If the current has carried you on to a smooth wall skirting the outside of the bend, lift the upstream edge (nearest the inside of the bend) and let your shoulder skid along the rock wall.

RUNNING THE WHOLE RAPID

Stage 1
Inspect the rapid.
● Note the hazards, if any.
● Decide on your line for the whole rapid.
● Memorize the lead-in.
● Memorize the broad movements through the rapid (moves left and right).
● Decide where you will stop – either breaks on the way through or after the difficulties.
● Note the rescue cover.

Stage 2
Gear check.
● Helmet secure.
● Buoyancy aid secure.
● Airbags inflated.
● Footrest correct.
● Take care putting the spraycover on.

Stage 3
The paddling.
● Bring the lead-in to mind and the line on the rapid.
● Set off.
● Keep your mind on the line well ahead. Let your body handle the immediate paddling.

Stage 4
How did it go?
● If you made a mistake, what was it?
● How could you improve the run?
Remember that every single paddling experience on white water, be it pleasant or less pleasant, makes you a better white-water paddler.

PACING THE RAPID

It is not necessary to paddle at a flat-out sprint for all of the rapid. It is likely that you would quickly exhaust yourself if you tried it. Pacing the rapid means finishing with a little energy left in reserve. The route through can involve drawing sideways, reverse ferry gliding, eddy turns, sprints through stopper holes, and powerful braces on

waves. Racing your way through the rapid detracts from the fun of stringing these moves together, quite apart from the fact that you are working at a speed that your mind cannot keep up with.

Letting the boat run
Watch a ball float through your rapid. It has an uncanny attraction for a good line through the obstacles. As you gain experience in handling your kayak, you learn that, just like the ball, it has a knack of taking itself along the right line. The idea of guiding the boat's general direction but leaving it alone where possible is called 'letting the boat run'. Beginners do it out of ignorance and survive some impressive passages through not interfering. Their success is the result of the 'If you don't know what to do, do nothing' theory and, although it proves the principle of letting the boat run, it is not putting it to its proper use.

A skilful paddler carefully lines up the kayak and then lets it go. This is economical in energy use and allows more time for the route ahead, checking on friends behind, or just feeling the movement of the water. Knowing when to pick up speed and drive the boat forwards is part of this approach. It is a controlled and safe style of running rapids allowing you to spend more time where you want to be – on white water.

Left: If, when you broadside on to a boulder or some other obstruction, you are slow in lifting the upstream edge of the kayak either before hitting the boulder or immediately afterwards, this is the result and the consequences for the paddler could be serious.

Right: If you are held in a side surf in a stopper, it is a good idea to rest for a moment to plan your way out. Of the three possible ways out, this photograph shows how the paddler in the blue kayak at the front of the trio exits out of the end of a stopper slot.

CHAPTER 5

ADVANCED WHITE-WATER PADDLING

Paddling water near or at the top end of the scale of difficulty has an inescapable seriousness to it. To quote Whit Deschener, 'The upper limit of kayaking depends solely on the individual's feelings about a short life'. It is intensity that makes kayaking at this level different from paddling on less difficult water. The turns are tighter, the boat moves faster, the rapids are longer, you get more frightened, and the jubilation of succeeding is ecstatic. It is not every paddler's cup of tea, and you should not see it as the logical pro-

gression from handling Grade IV water. When you get to the current absolute limit of difficulty in white water, the rivers fall into two quite different groups: those with a great deal of water and those with little water.

In the first case, huge rapids with enormous holes are run, causing paddler and kayak to spend a lot of time underwater. In the second type of river, there is much less water and, because it is usually falling very steeply or even vertically, the boat and occupant spend much of their

short paddling time in the air. At the moment, the rivers which fall into this very top category are few and far between in comparison to the vast number of extremely difficult rivers which offer a more balanced range of paddling.

The kayaker on this grade of water relies on the same basic techniques of white-water handling as

Heavy water on the Arkansas river in Colorado tosses the kayak on to its rear end.

ENDERS

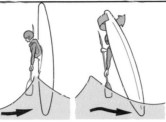

Start alongside the wave, facing upstream. Run the boat into the trough of the wave and steer straight into the current.

Let the nose get pulled under by the descending water. As the tail rises to the vertical, stand up on the footrest with your back on

the rear deck. From here, you can flip forwards, or reach for the water and use hip rotation to twist out to face downstream.

are needed for easier water but he or she must react more quickly, apply the techniques with greater precision, and possess an acute sense of anticipation of boat movement. A paddler working in big, heavy water must respond to the way the kayak is tossed around and flipped by the rapid. Freestyle kayaking is a good way to improve your boat control before tackling big rapids. In freestyling, you take a fixed piece of water and set yourself manoeuvres to test, improve, and develop your kayak handling.

ENDERS

Find a wave with a steep face and curling top and plenty of depth under it. Cross to the wave on a line level with it.
● Slide the kayak nose into the trough.
● Steer the boat square on to the wave using a stern rudder.
● Run the kayak deep into the trough by leaning forward, and hold it straight on the wave using alter-

Above left and left: A front ender. With the boat standing upright, stand on the footrest, reach into the water, and use hip rotation away from the blade to twist the boat out. You land upright and almost pointing downstream.

nate stern rudders.
● The nose of the boat suddenly pulls back under your feet and the boat comes upright.
On smallish waves, the ender stops here and the boat drops back on to its hull. You will, of course, have shot downstream in the process. On a larger wave, the kayak might continue to rotate after it is upright and you end up with a loop. The loop leaves you capsized and you tuck and roll up. The secret to a good ender is in running the kayak square down the wave face. When the boat suddenly stands on its nose, you can make the position last a little longer by standing straight on the footrest and pressing your head and shoulders against the rear deck. Remember to smile!

With the boat standing upright you can twist to land the kayak on its hull.
● Slow the ender by standing on the footrest.
● Reach into the water with a blade.
● Use a hip rotation away from the blade to twist the boat.
● You land upright and almost pointing downstream. Dry!

Backenders are harder to line up on waves but work quite well in stoppers. There is not much to do here. Your back will be in the water so it is a case of watching the bow to see if it wants to loop fully.

STOPPER WAVE SURFING

Find a good surface stopper wave.
• Get on and surf.
• Get in balance and try lifting the brace off the wave.
• Now drop the downstream hand into the stopper wave and gently scull to help you support.
• Try setting your paddles in the water on the upstream side of the kayak. Pick them up with the other hand as they pass under the hull.
• Now try handing your paddles over and surfing without them.
• Play a guitar, juggle oranges, or read this book! Very cool stuff!

WAVE RIDING

Now you need a good green wave face.
• Steer across the current until the kayak picks up the ramp of the wave.
• Straighten the boat on the wave using a stern rudder.
• Trim the boat on the wave by

altering your body position forwards or backwards until you reach a stable position that requires little or no paddling to hold.
• Remove the stern rudder and steer with a hand on that side.
• Juggle your paddle.
• Throw it away; steer with trailing hands.

RUNNING LARGE STANDING WAVES

Long lines of high standing waves are common on high-volume rivers. There is a critical speed at which the kayak will run in control over these waves. A speed which is slightly faster than the current is about right, and this will take you positively through the breaking tops. If you have to slow up in these waves, either to look around or to take a rest, it is useful to set the boat obliquely across the current. You will have to edge slightly downstream but it is more stable than drifting in line with the current leav-

ing you uncertain as to which side to brace on.

PADDLING SMALL DROPS

The majority of technically difficult white-water rivers contain small drops of up to about 2 metres (6.5 feet). This means that the drop is less than the length of most boats. 'Small' is a relative term, and sitting on the lip of a 2-metre drop for the first time is a moving experience for it seems a long way down. Being intimidated by the height is something you will overcome when you start devising tactics for shooting the fall.

Before you get into the kayak there are several things which you need to find out:
• Is the landing shallow or deep?
• How serious is the stopper underneath the drop?

The answer to the first question will help with the second. If the pool into which the water is pouring is obviously shallow, then it is unlikely

Left: Alan Fox running enormous white-water waves on the potentially hazardous Zambezi river, southern Africa.

Above: Before you get into the kayak, you should always find out: shallow or deep landing? how strong is the stopper?

that the stopper will give you any problems because the recirculating action of the vertical eddy cannot establish itself.

The landing
While the absence of a serious stopper is reassuring, the shallow water poses new problems. If the front of your kayak bottoms out as you come over the drop, there is a danger that you will stick solidly on the fall. If you cannot unhook the nose from the river bed you have got problems.

A medium-volume kayak on a 2-metre (6.5-foot) fall needs approximately 2 metres (6.5 feet) of depth to clear the bottom. This, of course, varies according to the weight of the paddler, aeration of water, and speed of the boat.

Testing for depth
You will often be uncertain about the amount of depth, and you can attempt to test it by using one of these methods:

● Paddle up to the drop from downstream and probe with your paddle. Your paddle can be used to estimate depth – it is approximately 2 metres (6.5 feet) long. *Do not attempt this if you are in any doubt about the stopper.*
● Find a long, light piece of tree from the forest floor; trim it into a pole and probe with that from the bank. Use your throw bag tied off as a handline to lie off. As you probe, as well as gauging depth, feel for the shape and nature of the river bed at the landing point. Is it boulders, gravel, creviced bedrock? Probe the area extensively in case there is a large isolated boulder, pillar, or ledge.
● If you simply cannot reach the landing spot or there are no trees, you can tie a rope off on the paddle shaft and throw the paddles in javelin style. Go gently at first; I once broke the blade of a new set of paddles doing this. If you have a set of split paddles, assemble them and use them for the job. Systematically

cover as much of the landing area as you can possibly reach.

Knowing the river bed formation under a drop is important, and paddlers often check out whole sections of river in dry conditions to get this kind of information. Time spent on this type of reconnaissance work can be invaluable to you on your first attempt on the river. If you know the landing of a drop to be shallow but with smooth, downstream sloping rock you can risk a glancing blow on the front of the boat if you are sure it can take it.

To reduce the depth of the boat's plunge:
● Paddle fast over the drop to give a flatter landing; or:
● Take off slightly angled to the fall so that the kayak falls more on its downstream edge than its nose. Avoid this one if there is doubt about the stopper.

The stopper
Making decisions about stoppers is never easy. The more experience

you have of inspecting and paddling them, the greater are your chances of getting it right. There is a number of points to consider.

• The back tow. How far does it extend from the base of the drop? If it is anything like a boat's length, it will be an extremely powerful current and you would be lucky to paddle out of it.

• The volume of water. If there is a lot of water thundering over the drop you must assume the stopper to be nasty.

• The depth. It is possible for the plunge pool to be deep enough for a stopper to form but shallow enough to allow a kayak to bottom out. Once your kayak's nose has hit the bottom, the rear will swing around and drop you into the teeth of the stopper slot. I once saw this happen because a paddler simply did not accelerate off the lip of the fall.

• Any weaknesses in the stopper slot where the current might be pushing a jet through. This is the place to land but you might have difficulty lining up perfectly because you cannot see over the drop. Use sighting marks on the bank or a paddler standing downstream to guide you.

If you are in doubt about a stopper, the only safe action is to leave it alone. If a paddler decides to run the drop then he should wait until you have set up good rescue cover. You then signal for him to come on.

Skirting the stopper

One way to improve your chances on a drop where the stopper is nasty is to take a fast line which lands you beyond the edge of the stopper slot. This works well and is quite feasible on many drops.

• Make a few powerful strokes to build speed.

• Have a blade on the lip to shoot the kayak into the air.

• Hold the landing stroke blade poised.

• The boat and blade land on the water.

Jumping the stopper below a small drop on the so-called 'Sock-em-dog' rapid, Chattooga river, in the United States.

• Shoot the boat forward out of the pool.

With experience you will develop a natural rhythm of strokes for small drops. This rhythm is a sign that you are acquiring skill. Habits in your technique will develop with surprisingly little conscious effort. Your mind is free to concentrate on ensuring that the line is correct and on what the next section looks like.

Rivers in which rough water is mainly the result of bedrock rather than boulders give superb paddling at all levels of difficulty. Some of the rivers of North Wales run in a series of smallish drops spaced with calm pools. These are frequently in small gorges canopied with a veil of branches. In autumn, the shafts of sunlight filtered by the roof of leaves fill the gorges with red and yellow

Above: Sue Dixon on the exit of 'the Pipeline' rapid, in the Conway Gorge in Wales.

Below and right: François Cirotteau on one of his most impressive conquests.

air. Where the drop is channelled in a narrow, rocky shoot, keep the paddles high and use the rock to brace on.

JUMPING A SMALL DROP

Above and right: Accelerate up to the lip and drive off with a single, hard stroke. In the air, set up your next stroke which drives you forward as soon as you can reach water. If you do not clear the stopper, get the power on.

Large drops

The three phases to paddling a large drop are: the lead-in and take-off; the fall or slide; the landing.

The middle phase is the one that sets these larger drops aside from the smaller ones. During this time, the kayak is falling under the influence of gravity and the paddler can do little to help the situation. The existence of this waiting period changes the rules of the game a little. Some would say it reduces kayaking to a case of simply having the nerve to hurl yourself over the edge and that the only skill is in listening for the bump at the bottom. In my opinion, this is a rather naive viewpoint, but the paddler contemplating jumping waterfalls is undoubtedly taking different things into account from the paddler in big water.

The kayak's flight:
• A kayak allowed to drift slowly over a vertical drop will quickly swing nose down.
• Launching at speed takes the kayak into a less vertical landing position which decreases the depth of the plunge.

Even though it might be preferable to launch off the lip at speed, some take-offs forbid this because of shallow ground on the lip or because the lead-in is so intricate. You have no choice then but to fall steeply. If the depth of the pool at the bottom is a problem, or if the exit from the landing pool is on one side, the boat can be angled on the lip so that you land more on your side. The ideal landing after a drop is to enter the plunge pool nose first and for the kayak to rise out of the water nose first.

On steep drops, with little water for the boat to ride on, the kayak tends to fall very steeply indeed and this causes it to rebound and jump backwards out of its plunge. Low-volume kayaks or those with little rocker are very prone to this. Shooting backwards towards the drop is not exactly a reassuring feeling. Once, it happened to me at the base of a 7-metre (23-foot) fall, and I was deposited into the very stopper

Above: Without speed on take-off, the kayak drops into the vertical. Below: At speed, the boat clears obstructions.

Above: An angle landing is much shallower. This might be useful if the plunge pool lacks depth. Watch out for the stopper. Below: Landing square to the drop is easiest to control. Watch out for the rebound into the fall.

which I was confident the drop would take me through.

Water movement at the base of the fall

Water falling vertically into a deep pool is normally the formula for a nasty stopper. The formation at the base of waterfalls, however, is often found to release a kayak and paddler very easily.

Two factors have a bearing on this.

1 The falling kayak dives deeply into the recirculation and often reaches the water escaping downstream from the effect of the stopper. This is also seen when medium- or low-volume kayaks appear to pass untouched through large surface stoppers which hold higher-volume boats. This, however, is not a cast-iron case for using lower-volume kayaks on drops because the danger of entrapment from a deep plunge is as big a danger as being held by a stopper.

2 The height which the water is falling through causes it to disperse or to fan out and hit the plunge pool over quite a large area. Remember it is the **volume** of the water in proportion to the drop that counts most. Increase the amount of water dramatically in almost any waterfall and, potentially, you have got a very dangerous stopper.

When the drop is not vertical but is a steep sloping slab, the water is concentrated as it hits the plunge pool and this creates a stopper with more holding power.

This is the process of getting afloat by dropping off a rock or sliding down a steep bank. It is similar to paddling drops in many ways and

The largest of three successive drops – 5 metres (16½ feet), 7 metres (23 feet), 4 metres (13 feet) – on the Travo in Corsica. The stopper on this drop is quite a holder. The plunge pool is very deep, and the less-than-vertical face of the fall keeps the water unaerated as it enters the pool, setting up a strong and deep circulation. The paddler's line clearly shows his plan to stay clear of the stopper.

can be used as a controlled way of letting paddlers familiarize themselves with plunge landings. It would be easy to think that seal launching is totally safe as long as the depth is adequate. This is not so. A bad landing can stun and hurt you, finishing the day before you have begun. My most memorable seal launch was in a gorge. I launched off a rock ledge and dropped about 5 metres (16 feet) into 'solid' water. The impact ripped the lining out of my helmet leaving my head inside a cavernous plastic shell which ceremoniously fell over my face.

Some river banks are so bouldery and craggy that it is impossible to get afloat by any other method. The great advantage of seal launching is that you can take time and care putting on the spray deck without worrying about drifting downstream or losing a paddle.

Once the spray deck is on, you push off with a blade on one side and a hand on the other. Launch forwards or sideways according to how deep you are prepared to go. Two landings are shown in the illustrations.

1 This can happen if you launch slowly off a bridge. The kayak's vertical fall generates further rotation and you meet the water face on.

2 This is extremely dangerous. There is a serious risk to the spine from the compression it experiences on impact.

Lowering yourself a metre or so on your hands can often reduce the height of the drop enough to give you a more controlled entry.

BAD LAUNCHES; BAD LANDINGS

1 A slow launch off a high platform can make an impression on you.

2 Landing square on to the hull from even a small height subjects your spine to serious compression forces. Do not risk this.

An abseil launch. Proper climbing equipment and ropes were used for this unusual descent into a gorge. The water was calm at the bottom and the paddler (the author) had gauged the rope length so that he could drop a short distance off the end of it into the pool. Many white-water adventures are enhanced by combining the skills and principles of other sports. Skis, horses, bicycles, and even microlight aircraft have been used to help paddlers get to the water.

EQUIPMENT FOR DROPS

Kayaks with finely pointed ends have no place on drops. The risk of snagging the sharp nose on rocks is high and the consequences can be extremely serious. Very short kayaks have further to fall than longer boats and this gives them more speed as they enter the water. They do, however, cope remarkably well with landings and on long rock slides their blunt noses and missing ends keep them from being slewed around by hooking projections on the rock.

Above: Seal launching is the technique used to get afloat by dropping off a rock or bank.

Footrests
The footrest is the single item of equipment which needs most attention. Clearly, its impact-absorption qualities are essential. One footrest system which I learned from a German canoeist used the stretching qualities of climbing rope to add 'give'. The buoyancy tank which forms the footrest in some kayaks is an ideal shock absorber. Pedal footrests can be modified temporarily

Above: Here a rope is being used to help with a more tricky launch to give a controlled entry.

by cutting sections of polyethylene foam which fit snugly against each pedal.

Knee padding
When a kayak impacts on its nose, either vertically or horizontally, the paddler has a tendency to slip forwards off the seat. This tends to drive the knees upwards into the braces and deck. Padding around this area reduces the risk of injury through a broken brace or pressure on the deck.

Nose cones
The point of a polyethylene kayak is particularly vulnerable to damage because it is not easy to mould extra thickness into that area. Some paddlers use replaceable nose cones, held on with bolts or self-tapping screws, to protect the end.

Helmets
Under normal circumstances, a canoeist's helmet serves mainly to protect him or her from underwater contact with rocks. More difficult paddling in shallow rivers means

IMPACT-ABSORBING FOOTREST SYSTEM

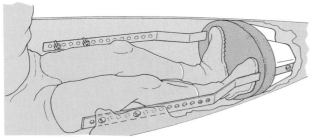

To prevent damage to the spine when going over a drop, use a well-designed impact-absorbing footrest system.

that impact and abrasion are possible on the surface when the paddler is moving fast. A good helmet is essential. A full-face helmet is the only sensible head covering when working in large, shallow drops.

Elbow pads

Where the paddling takes you through narrow constrictions, your elbows are vulnerable to knocks. Good elbow pads can save the paralysing numbness you get when you hit the bony points of the joint. Some steep mountain rivers are so densely strewn with boulders that you need to use them to turn on. The technique is called the **elbow turn** and requires some form of padding of the elbows.

• Guide the kayak broadside on to the boulder.
• Lift the upstream edge as you approach it.
Drop the near elbow on to the boulder and pull yourself in close to it.
Pivot the kayak forwards and downstream using the knees to drive as with the bow rudder.

Elbow turns can also be used to slow down your rate of descent on a steep section of water. It gives you a chance to look ahead and take a rest from the strenuous work of reverse ferry gliding.

INSPECTING RAPIDS

At this level of difficulty the rapids will either be very long or very complex or even both. Memorizing a detailed line is a daunting task. The obvious thing to do is to divide the rapid into sections which are separated by a resting place or obvious pull-out point. Do not be tempted to do your inspection from a high point, such as a bridge. If possible get down to bank level so that you can gauge the size of waves and drops and assess the water's speed.

• When you decide on your line, draw it on to a plan view of the rapid in your mind. Also go to the awkward bits and try to get a canoeist's-eye view of them so that you will recognize the parts as you come to them.

• Go somewhere on your own, close your eyes, and paddle the

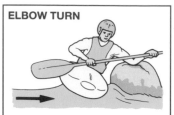

ELBOW TURN

Plastic kayaks have opened up new ground. In tight, steep boulder fields, the rocks function as turning posts and resting spots.

rapid. Do it in order and make the break-outs where you intend to rest.
• Check out anything that you are unsure about.
• Do another couple of mental runs. See yourself doing the whole rapid as you planned it.

Once you have decided on rescue cover, go to the kayak and check:
• Airbags.
At the water's edge check:
• Helmet and buoyancy aid.
• Go afloat and paddle around to warm up. Stretch and rotate your trunk.
• Go when the bank team signal you to.

When you memorize a line do not try to store too much detailed information in your mind; just remember the main route. With practice you will improve your recall ability. Making sketches when you first check out the river is an excellent way to get a line that you are going to follow into your head.

STAYING IN CONTROL

Fear plays an important part in white-water paddling. It functions as a control mechanism, preventing you from tackling things which are beyond your capabilities. Fear can also take a powerful hold on you when you have chosen to run something having weighed up the problems and decided that it is within your scope. Under these conditions, the apprehension you experience keys you up and helps you to paddle better.

The graph of stress against performance is common to many sporting situations. It shows that

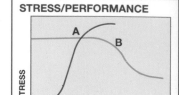

STRESS/PERFORMANCE

Fear can raise your stress level to a point where your performance falls off dramatically.

stress causes an improvement in performance up to a critical point (Point B). Beyond this, however, you 'go over the top' and there is a drastic reduction of your performance level. People sometimes refer to the feeling as being 'psyched out'. So, if you are getting ready to paddle a piece of unfamiliar water, you must try to reduce the stress level when you feel it rising to beyond your Point-B level. You can do this simply by making yourself relax. There are many methods for doing this; some would relax you to such an extent that you would fall asleep – definitely not what you want! Try this simple method of calming yourself.

• Get into the boat and put on the spray deck.
• Before you set off, close your eyes.
• Rest your arms on the spray deck.
• Breathe in.
• Breathe out slowly and deeply, letting yourself sink deeply into the seat.
• Again, and then once more.
• As you breathe out, think only of letting your arms sink on to the spray deck and let your shoulders sag.
• Now you will feel steadier and ready to go.

You must, of course, practise this to get used to it. At first, you will not know just how 'psyched up' to let yourself become, and it is always possible that you are the kind of person who does not need to wind down at all. Whichever is the case, start the rapid only with positive thoughts in your head.

ROLLING

It is absolutely essential that you are able to roll confidently on white water if you are to have any safety reserve. The paddler on extreme white water which falls into the shallow and rocky category must, however, also be prepared not to roll. There are circumstances in these rivers where the risk attached to staying under and attempting to roll is greater than getting out of the kayak fast and going for shore. Such circumstances are not easy to define but narrow, rocky channels

with drops are the kinds of places where the paddler dare not allow his or her head to get below the boat. At times like this, safety cockpits are clearly advantageous, allowing the paddler to step clear of the kayak often without even getting a wet head.

Whether you attempt to roll in a rapid or take to the water is not a decision to be left until things go wrong. In these moments, the mind is rarely able to reason clearly, and the chances are that you will make the wrong choice. The time to decide your tactics and make your

It is essential that the white-water paddler has the ability to roll. Equally essential is the ability to decide not to roll.

decisions is when you inspect a rapid or fall. You should discuss your intentions with the bank support team or rescue cover so that they are able to get you out quickly if your choice is to swim. I must emphasize that this is not an argument for having no rolling skill. You must be able to roll so that you have the choice of actions.

CHAPTER 6

TRAINING FOR WHITE WATER

The concept of training for any sport means a planned, systematic procedure which will bring about an improvement in performance. It could be that, as a non-competitor, you consider yourself free from the bonds of training schedules, more of a wanderer than a highly trained athlete. Your kayaking alone will be perfect for keeping a good level of fitness. If, on the other hand, you have decided that you want to improve as a kayak paddler and tackle more difficult water, then you must prepare and train yourself with the same determination and commitment as any competitive sportsperson.

The training falls initially into two main categories:
1 Technique training.
2 Fitness training.

In technique training, you are developing your boat handling, river reading, and reaction time. Some of this training needs to be structured, in which you set yourself specific tasks while, at other times, you are improving by virtue of the circumstances. Paddling safe rapids on sight is a good example of the latter type of training.

'THE FEEL OF WATER'

One of the important factors which determine whether or not a person will become a good swimmer is an innate ability to sense the limbs driving against the water. Exactly the same 'feel of the water' is required for kayaking except that your arms have extensions to them – the paddle blades. Because we are not born with paddles in our arms, we must learn this sensation of the water through the shaft from practice. Through your paddling, you will acquire this feel gradually, and training on technique will speed that along.

BASIC FREESTYLE TRICKS

Freestyle practice is one of the most enjoyable forms of training for white water. Working in pairs or groups helps you to judge yourself and also

to get out and do it when you might otherwise not bother.

In some parts of the world, 'freestyling' or 'hotdogging' competitions are run, in which the paddler is judged on the use of a small section of rapid containing holes and waves. Freestyle tricks are built around three basic manoeuvres: stopper surfing, enders, and wave riding. Of these, the stopper surfing provides the foundation for the others.

The paddler starts with the kayak held sideways in the grip of the stopper. The first move is to demonstrate control of balance by holding the boat on edge and taking your weight off the brace. Start by simply lifting the bracing blade off the water, and then try letting go of the shaft with the downstream hand. Plunge it deeply into the water beside the boat where you can feel the pressure of the downstream current. This gives considerable support but looks to the uninitiated as though you have magical

powers. (Attracting bystanders' attention is part of freestyling so do not feel inhibited about it.) What you do next to test your control and balance is limited only by how vivid your imagination is. Singing 'Home on the Range' while using your paddle for guitar accompaniment is a good starting point! A lazy, 'Don't rush me' expression is almost essential to create the right atmosphere, but juggling oranges, smoking a cigar, or Rubic's Cubing are really for the 'smoothies'.

Below: The ender is one of the three basic starting positions for various aerial freestyle tricks. Stopper surfing and wave riding are also used to build around.

Right: Side-surfing comfortably in a stopper slot. The river is in Norway. The song is 'Home on the Range'! You will attract the attention of the uninitiated so do not be put off.

The next stopper manoeuvre is the '360'. This time you push the front of the kayak out of the stopper slot leaving the rear half firmly in its grip. Another little push and it slams back into the stopper slot, facing in the opposite direction from the starting position. You quickly transfer the edging at the mid-point in the turn. To complete the 360, the same manoeuvre is repeated but leading with the rear end of the kayak. Once you have developed the knack of pulling the end of the boat out of the grip of the stopper, the secret in the 360 is to change the edging at just the right time. Short kayaks are excellent for carrying out fast, continuous 360s which look very cool to the observer.

Finally, on stopper surfing, make sure you choose a wave which has enough depth of water. An accidental, upstream capsize happens extremely quickly and it is best if there is no sharp edge close to the surface on which to put your helmet to the test.

Stopper surfing can be linked to riding green waves, enders and to pop-outs. In a pop-out, the kayak is driven skywards from the classic 'ender' position by the combined buoyancy of the boat and pressure of water in the wave. A pop-out is colloquially considered 'cosmic' when the whole boat becomes airborne and its 'pilot' can be heard screeching and hooting hysterically many kilometres downstream. If you can run the kayak down the ramp of a wave deep into the trough and hold a controlled, rearward pop-out, starting a twist as it leaves the water so that it lands on its hull while you maintain an expression of total boredom, you will become a cult hero or heroine overnight.

SET MANOEUVRES

Set yourself specific moves on small sections of rapid and repeat the moves, experimenting with angles, lean, and stroke timing. Now string the manoeuvres together and use more of the rapid. Do not be afraid to go into a flat-water pool and rehearse stroke movements and sequences, and then go back into the rapid. Also try new moves, such as the eddy line draw. Eddy hopping

These steep and cleanly formed standing waves contain more than enough energy to stand a kayak on its nose even though they are not particularly large.

back upstream is good technical training and lets you recover a little, while you think about the last run on white water.

SHORT KAYAKS

If you can fit into a short kayak, borrow one from time to time and go on some waves in it. Let the waves capsize you so that you do a lot of rolls. Learn the half roll.
● Lift your head out of the water and take a breath.
● Fall back under in tucked position.
● Set up the paddle carefully.
● Roll.
This gives you air when you have been capsized, after you have had your chest flattened, or when you have simply not had a chance to take a breath. Broken storm surf is good practice for this too!

TEACHING OTHERS

Less-experienced paddlers need and want guidance, and they will appreciate it from you. Teaching others gives you a better understanding of the techniques and skills of kayak handling and, in turn, enhances your own paddling. It also consolidates the close bond between white-water kayakers, and reminds us all that we carry a responsibility for each other as well as for ourselves.

FITNESS TRAINING

Medical researchers who have studied kayaking in terms of human movement are impressed by the intensity of the work which is carried out by the upper body of a paddler. Moving your body using only one-third of its total muscle mass has been described by exercise physiologists as 'running with your arms'. It is considered by some to be second only to cycle racing as an exercise for developing the heart muscle. What this tells us, in fact, is that kayaking is hard work. I am sure we already know this, so what better case can you have for improving your fitness?

There are three essential elements of fitness.
● Flexibility.
● Local muscular endurance.
● Muscle strength and speed.

Flexibility
Kayaking will develop your upper-body strength whether you like it or not. This is accompanied by a slight loss in muscular flexibility. Good kayaking technique requires a high degree of mobility in your trunk, hips, shoulders, and wrists, however, and this means gaining more flexibility, rather than losing it. Consider trunk rotation alone. How many times has it been referred to in the previous chapters? It plays a part in just about every kayaking action. Maintaining and improving your range of trunk rotation will greatly help your paddling. You develop flexibility by regular, progressive stretching exercises. Stretching is a science and an art in itself, and there are fundamental principles which you must understand before you begin any exercises.

When to stretch?
● Daily.
● Before and after training or paddling sessions.
● When you feel stiff.

Why stretch?
● It reduces muscle tension.
● It prevents injury (a strong, pre-stretched muscle resists stress better than a strong, unstretched muscle).
● It increases the range of movement.

Stretching exercises should never be painful, and bouncing or overstretching are counterproductive. Make sure that you do not stretch beyond the comfortable limits of your own body and that, when you hold a stretch, you only feel 'mild tension' in the muscle or muscles involved. When you are well used to a particular stretching exercise, then you can hold it for periods of about 30 seconds but, to begin with, you should not hold a position for such a prolonged time.

Overleaf is a simple stretching routine. Use this routine regularly so that you memorize the exercises, and learn to get into the correct position for each one. It takes a little practice to be able to settle into the positions straight away. Remember always to stretch within your limits of comfort and, if you have suffered a shoulder dislocation or any other injury, you should seek medical advice before attempting the shoulder stretches or other stretches.

Local muscular endurance
When you make a single forward paddle stroke, you apply a force of between 9 and 14 kilograms (20 to 30 pounds) to the blade. Think how many times you do that in a single paddling session, and it becomes clear why you require local muscular endurance.

Some of the work which you do in the kayak involves maintaining relatively easy movements over a prolonged period. Paddling long, easy stretches of water on a river journey is an example of this. This kind of muscle activity is classed as **aerobic** and is fuelled by oxygen carried in the blood. Some people, such as good marathon runners, are endowed with a physical

---

THE 360

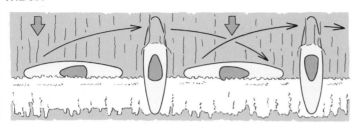

Start by side surfing in balance close to the end of the stopper. Push the nose into the current so that you start to climb out. Leave the tail in the slot so that the kayak is sucked backwards into it. A little forward sweep drops you back into the side surf on the other side. Repeat the turn by pushing the tail out first.

THE POP-OUT

A good straight ender and the right size of wave can get you airborne.

NINE STRETCHES FOR PADDLERS

Right: Start with your legs bent under you. Reach forward and press down slightly with your palms. Feel the tension on your sides and arms but do not strain. Hold for fifteen seconds. Do it one arm at a time if you prefer it. This exercise stretches the powerful lateral muscles which are used extensively in paddling.

Above: Another shoulder stretch is to try to join your fingers behind your back. Hold this position for ten to fifteen seconds. If your hands do not meet, have someone pull them towards each other – very gently.

Another method is to hold a towel and gradually move your hands together. If you have had any form of shoulder injury, such as a dislocations, you should miss out this one. Shoulder dislocations are relatively common injuries for white-water paddlers. How they occur and how they may be treated are dealt with in more detail on page 105.

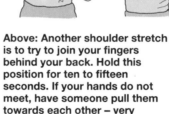

Above: This forearm and wrist stretch is excellent after a long day's paddle. Support yourself on knees and hands, fingers towards knees. Keep the palms flat, and rock gently back to feel the stretch.

Above: Start with the soles of your feet together and hold on to your toes. Gently pull yourself forwards from the hips until you feel a stretch in your groin. Hold for thirty seconds. These groin muscles help you to grip the kayak through the thigh braces, and so they work very hard in white-water paddling.

Above: Sit with the right leg stretched. Bend the left leg, cross the left foot over and rest it to the outside of the knee. Bend the right elbow and rest it on the outside of the upper left thigh.

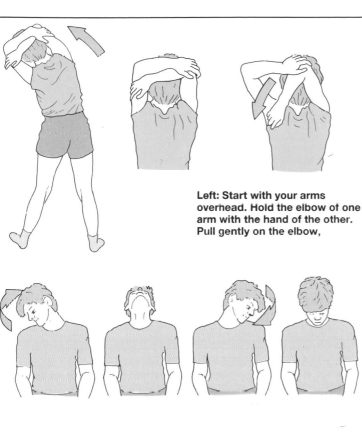

creating a stretch in your upper arm and side of your trunk. Do this slowly and without jerking. Hold for fifteen seconds. This stretch can be done while walking. A variation is to bend sideways from standing, maintaining the elbow pressure.

Always stretch both sides; do not hold your breath, and remember that stretching done correctly is not painful. You will soon develop a feeling for correct stretching and learn what is right for *your* body.

Left: Start with your arms overhead. Hold the elbow of one arm with the hand of the other. Pull gently on the elbow,

Left: Start with your head on its side creating a stretch on the side of your neck. Roll your head slowly forwards and on to the other side. Return gently to the start, applying stretch where it feels tight. Rock your head back to stretch the front of the neck and then forwards to the starting position. Try the neck stretch while resting in the boat.

Left: Lie on your back with your arms extended overhead and your legs out straight. Stretch out with your arms and fingers and also with your legs and toes. Hold for five seconds and then relax. Repeat as often as you like. This stretches the muscles of the rib cage, abdominals, spine, shoulders, and arms.

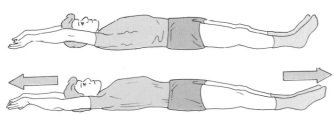

Right: Start by sitting with a straight, outstretched leg and the sole of the other foot touching the inside of the thigh. Bend forwards from the hips until you feel the stretch under the outstretched thigh (the hamstrings). The kayaking position can create shortened hamstrings and this stretch will keep them flexible so that they do not limit your forward lean.

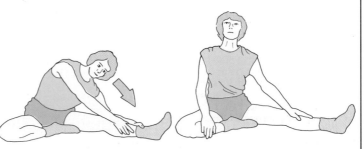

make-up which is particularly suited to this form of exercise. The nature of white-water paddling, however, is such that you find yourself suddenly working much harder, accelerating through waves, powering the boat around turns, and side-slipping. This kind of muscular activity is known as **anaerobic** exercise. The fuel supply this time comes from a chemical process which does not require oxygen although oxygen is used at a later stage. The process produces the chemical substance, lactic acid, and the paddler eventually experiences an 'oxygen deficit'. You feel weak and start to gasp or pant.

Most white-water paddling keeps you working in both systems, high on the scale of aerobic activity and with bursts of activity in the anaerobic range. Your training will have to take both of these into account. The sessions can be in the boat and on land. The variation helps to keep you interested, and the land training allows you to keep going when dry weather, short days, or frozen water prevent you from getting afloat.

To train in the kayak for aerobic work, make use of long continuous exercise sessions, including periods of surfing, polo matches, long paddles at steady speed on easy water. Inland or sea touring is an ideal form of endurance training.

For anaerobic work, train by making 30, 40, or 50-second bursts around a course which you set on the rapids. Follow each burst with a recovery period when you paddle very gently. For example, try break-outs and crosses down through the rapid for 30 seconds and then paddle gently back to start – taking about 1 minute. Then repeat the course. Or, do four 30-second bursts with 1 minute between each, followed by a short rest; four more 30-second bursts and a short rest, and so on.

Land-based endurance training includes: swimming long distances; cross-country skiing; circuit training; some running; light weight training using high repetitions for each exercise; paddling machine.

It is possible to work out training regimes which involve very tough work loads using a paddling machine but it is worth guarding against possible boredom by training in groups or by listening to music while you train. You can undertake long training sessions of between fifteen minutes and half-an-hour of steady work or, for anaerobic work, up to 40-second bursts followed by gentle recovery. You should simply regulate the intervals as you would with your boat work.

Circuit training is another means of developing fitness and endurance. The circuit includes a range of low-skill exercises stationed around a gymnasium or field. Set a number of repetitions for each exercise and mark it at the station. Use low loads in the exercises and have about six or eight exercises. Do three circuits. The whole should last between twelve and fifteen minutes. Exercises could include: press-ups; sit-ups with bent legs; squat thrusts; alternate punching upward with light, hard weights; bent-forward alternate rowing as above; two sprints.

For anaerobic benefits use more body weight exercises such as chins and bar dips with gentle, active recovery periods between. If you become involved in weight training, use light weights only, doing fifteen to twenty repetitions, and work in circuits.

Muscle strength

A white-water paddler requires considerable strength in the musculature of the arms, shoulders, chest, and back. Once again, it is useful to develop strength both on and off the water.

To improve your strength by training in the kayak, there is a number of exercises you can practise:
- Tow a drag, such as a car tyre, behind the boat on flat water.
- Paddle with oversized blades which give enormous resistance in the water.
- Paddle a flat-water course consisting of sharp turns, fast side slips,

The paddling machine provides good endurance training when it is too cold or too dry to paddle on the river. Music, or the presence of others, makes the training a little easier.

STRENGTHENING YOUR ABDOMEN

Kayakers require considerable strength in the abdominal area to transmit effort into the pelvis and logo.

Sit-ups strengthen these muscles. The knees should always be raised throughout this exercise or there will be a risk of lower back strain. Holding the arms up makes the exercise harder as does inclining the surface on which you are working. These are ways of increasing the load as you get stronger. Rotating to touch the elbows to the opposite knees on each sit-up is even more like the paddling movement.

Above: Curls. Starting position, feet apart, and holding the bar under-grasp.

Above right: Curls. Middle position. Flex your arms slowly, to bring the bar up until it reaches your chest, breathing in as you do. From this position, you lower the bar slowly.

and tight staggered turns.
● As above but using a heavy, slower-turning kayak.

All of these exercises demonstrate that the principle behind strengthening a muscle is to overload it, in other words, you ask it to contract against resistance exceeding that normally encountered. The muscle is forced to work to its full capacity or what is known as 'maximally'. These maximal or near-maximal contractions stimulate growth and adaptations in the tissues which lead to increased strength.

On land, the use of a multigym or free weights gives you the means to continue to increase the overload as muscle strength improves. This *progressive* increase is essential in a strength training programme. If you do not have access to weight training equipment, then you should use your own body weight as the resistance and increase that resistance with a diver's weight belt, for example. The exercises which you should use are:
1 Chins – using normal paddle grip.
2 Press-ups – increase the weight on arms by raising your feet on a bench.

3 Diagonal sit-ups.
4 Dips – between parallel bars.

If you have not used free weights before, you should obtain guidance or do further reading before trying it because it is quite possible to injure yourself through poor technique or mishandling of the equipment. Always warm up with gentle exercise before starting a session with weights. When you are sweating, do your stretching routine and then start the weight training. Here are some exercises useful for kayaking:
Curl
Stand with your feet apart.
Hold the bar under-grasp.
Slowly flex your arms until the bar reaches your chest.
Lower the bar slowly.
Breath in as you lift – out as you lower. Keep your back straight.

BENCH PRESS

The bench press is a good general strengthener for the upper body and specifically develops the muscles which  straighten the arms as well as some in the shoulders. Reverse strokes, bow pulls, and stern ruddering use these muscles.

Bench press
Lie on the bench with your feet on the ground.
Take the weight on your outstretched arms above your chest using the normal grip that you would use on your paddle.
Lower the bar to your chest.
Press to straighten your arms.
Breathe in when lowering – out as arms straighten.

Single arm rowing (dumb bell)
With one knee and hand on the bench, and your trunk parallel to the floor, pull the weight to your side using arm flex and trunk rotation, and then lower.

Multigym weight-training equipment is much safer to use because you cannot overbalance or drop weights. It is still possible for injury to occur through bad technique so you should take the same amount of care.

Down pulls
Kneel below the horizontal pulley bar.
Hold the handles at arm's reach.
Pull the bar to behind your neck.
Return to the start position, or
Pull to your chest.

These exercises approach the kind of movements made by the paddler in the kayak.

To start with, set a weight which allows you to do twelve repetitions. Once your technique has improved a little, use six to eight repetitions and do three sets of each exercise. Use the same order of exercises on each workout day, and set days two or three times a week.

Single arm rowing using a dumbell. With one hand and knee on the bench, grasp the dumbell.

Seated military press
Start with the bar resting across the shoulders. Push to full arm extension and lower slowly.

Isokinetic machines are excellent for reproducing the kayak paddling movements. They work on a pulley system which gives them a lot of flexibility. It is even possible to attach a paddle shaft to some machines. The resistance of the pulleys is variable over quite a wide range.

Muscle speed
The fibres which make up our muscles are of two distinct types: 'fast-

Pull the weight to your side using arm flex and trunk rotation, and then lower.

twitch' muscle fibres are quick firing, capable of fast contractions, but fatigue easily; 'slow-twitch' fibres are long running giving slow contractions, but they keep going longer. Naturally, the fast-twitch fibres produce the high-speed movements, such as reacting with a brace. Your training, both on land and on the water, should work the fast-twitch fibres.

In the boat, speed-training exercises should include paddling short, very fast bursts for 10 to 15 seconds with long recovery periods (a minute). On land, isokinetic machines and conventional pad-

DOWN PULLS	SEATED MILITARY PRESS	

This action is very close to many kayaking movements.	A shoulder and arm straightening exercise. Have a	partner standing in to help if you get out of control.

dling machines provide good speed training. Use medium to low resistances for short, fast repetitions. Simple exercises such as chins, sit-ups, and press-ups, again in fast bursts, are good for developing speed and endurance.

A PRE-PADDLING WARM-UP ROUTINE

One of the habits you should get into is to establish a routine for getting afloat. Tennis players provide good models. Before every serve, a top tennis player re-enacts an almost absurd routine of ball bouncing, head wiping, and twitching. Each time it happens in the same order.

This performs several functions:
1 By causing things to happen almost subconsciously it makes sure that you do not forget anything.
2 It 'cues in' your mind on the task, bringing you to the right level of concentration, and blocking out distractions.

Perhaps you do not see the connection between you paddling a boat and a championship tennis player. Some day you will feel the same desire to create the right actions as the tennis player has before the serve and you will be glad that you have developed a warm-up routine to increase your chances. The routine is developed around equipment you have to check,

memorizing the route, calming yourself, and warming up your body.

The warm-up
Cold muscles have a greater viscosity than warm muscles. You do more work, in other words, if you paddle with unwarmed muscle and also you increase the risk of injuring a muscle through strain. You can do your warming up on land or in the boat. Some of your warm up, at least, should be in the boat because it helps to tune in your skills.

It is always tempting, especially when you are anxious, to cut the warm-up and get paddling. At these times, try to take control and stick to your usual routine preparation.

LAND WARM-UP	BOAT WARM-UP
 	**1. Trunk rotation swings with the paddles in air. Start gently and increase the range of the swings.** **2. Shoulder stretch as for land warm-up.** **3. Short bursts of rapid paddling.**

1. Bend forward and freely rotate the trunk with arm swings.

2. Rotate the arms front and rearwards in opposite directions.

3. Hold the paddle at the blade joints and above the head. Press the shaft rearwards and stretch the shoulders.

CHAPTER 7

SAFETY AND RESCUE

So long as humans have to breathe air, it will never be possible to make white-water kayaking entirely safe. The paddler's aim is to enjoy the river and minimize the risk by good preparation and cautious behaviour. Being as safe as possible takes many considerations into account and asks the question, 'Is the right person in the right place with the right equipment at the right time?' The individual paddler is central to the whole thing and it is his or her **desire to be safe** which will be put to test on the river.

Here are some of the questions which have to be answered truthfully by the paddler.

● Have your experience and your knowledge combined to give you good **judgement**?
● Are you **skilful** enough to tackle this?
● Are you at the level of **fitness** necessary?
● Has the **decision** to paddle been entirely your own?
● Are you in the right **state of mind** to paddle this?
● Do you understand the **hazards** in this section?
● Is your **kayak** as safe as it can possibly be made for this water?
● Is your **personal equipment** suitable?
● Are you equipped for an **emergency**?

If you have answered 'No' to any of these questions, then you must question your **desire to be safe**.

PERSONAL SAFETY AND RESCUE EQUIPMENT

The following items are simple, multifunction tools which the white-water paddler should consider part of the equipment: karabiner; knife; throw-bag. They should live with your kayaking clothing so that you do not go anywhere without them.

Karabiner
This is an oval-shaped link used in mountaineering and rock climbing for rope connections. It has many uses for the paddler including attaching a rope to a boat's grab handle, holding equipment into a kayak, and as a pulley in hauling systems. Alloy karabiners are preferable to steel because they will not rust and are considerably lighter. Some have a locking sleeve which screws over the gate when the karabiner is closed. These are mostly unsuitable for white-water use because grit can clog them and the few seconds needed to unscrew the gate bites deeply into time in emergencies. Paddlers carry karabiners on the shoulder of a buoyancy aid, on a tape sling around the waist, or clipped on to a

throw-bag. One is useful, but carrying two karabiners is better.

Knife
You should never take a rope on the river with you unless you have a knife to cut it. The life-saving rope can turn into a deadly snare within seconds, and the only solution can be to cut it. Your knife has a multitude of other uses, not all of which are life saving. Keep it sharp and oil the spring regularly so that you can open the blade with cold hands.

Throw-bag
The throw-bag is a store of rope, for all sorts of uses, which is compact and secure. It is also the means by which you get a rescue line to a swimmer in a rapid. It does both jobs superbly but its successful handling demands practice and familiarity from its owner.

The rope **must** be: floating; visible; a minimum of 9 millimetres (⅓ inch) diameter; made of a soft material; no less than 1000 kilograms (2200 pounds) breaking strain; and limp to allow it to lie easily in the bag. Its diameter and the material from which it is made affect its ease of handling. Braided rope works best in throw-bags. The fact that it soaks up water makes it better for throwing because of the increased weight. Keep a small loop

---

KARABINER

This simple piece of mountaineering equipment has many uses in kayaking. Its main function is to link ropes quickly and detach easily. Karabiners are used by paddlers for attaching ropes and slings (loops of strong nylon tape) to boats for various purposes. In emergencies, karabiners save time and can also perform as friction brakes or pulleys.

THROW-BAG

The throw-bag is the paddler's primary rescue tool. It should contain between 15 and 25 metres (50 to 80 feet) of floating rope and must be kept close.

OTHER EQUIPMENT

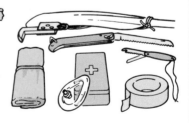

A selection of equipment you should carry with you at all times for reasons of safety and comfort. From top left to bottom right: paddle hook; saw; bivouac bag; first-aid kit; knife; tape.

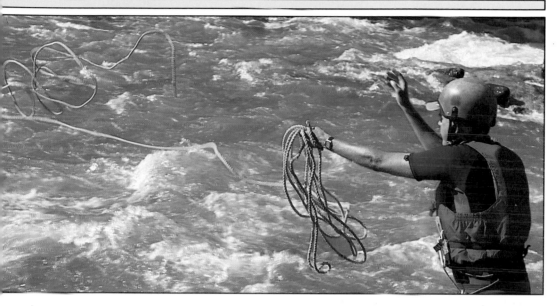

A system of throw-line in the conventional rope coil. In this case, the rope has been formed into two coils, giving the rescuer two chances to throw. In my opinion, the throw-bag is a better system but the rope coil is worth remembering as a stand-by.

knotted into the free end of the rope to take a karabiner and to function as a stopper to mark the rope's end.

The bag must be: visible – preferably yellow or orange; floating – or contain a small amount of foam flotation; tubular or slightly flared towards the opening – this makes it aerodynamic and causes the rope to 'load' properly; with an opening which will allow a fist into the bag – draw cords are not as good as the collar closure which forms a natural handle yet permits the neck to open completely; with a positive collar closure; with a rope loop or handle at its base; reasonably watertight.

When you come to throw the bag to a swimmer you will need the rope to pull easily from the bag. It must come out a piece at a time and not all at once or you will lose the weight of the rope which is so important for

carrying it to the target. The bag is loaded, therefore, by feeding in the rope from the bag end towards the free end. It should *not* be coiled nor picked up in random handfuls and stuffed in no matter how rushed you might be, or it will snag itself when you throw it.

Take care of the throw-bag and keep it loaded correctly for a throw. When you need it you will have little enough time to get it ready for use.

Other personal equipment

This equipment will depend on the kind of area you are working in, or whether you are part of a group, on the climate, and on any leadership responsibilities you might have.

If you are paddling a wilderness river or one which runs through a gorge, a pair if **split paddles** could make the difference between finishing the trip and leaving your kayak for a wild climb out. The paddles fit neatly under the airbags with the blades nearest the cockpit area.

A **bivouac bag** is a strong polythene or nylon bag which gives basic shelter in the event of an accident. Made from orange material, it is useful for signalling and can also make an improvized stretcher.

It is worth carrying a simple first-

aid kit to provide the basic first-aid treatment for bleeding, a fracture, or other relevant, specific problems such as sunburn, insect bite, or diarrhoea. A basic kit could include: wound dressing; adhesive dressing strip; non-allergent adhesive tape; triangular bandage; elastic roller bandage; two non-stick gauze dressing pads; painkillers; scissors; tweezers; four large safety pins.

SPARE CLOTHING

The amount and type of any spare clothing you take depend entirely on how good your kayak clothing is and how extreme is the cold, but you might well include nylon windproofs to cover wetsuit legs; and a fibrepile or woollen sweater and woollen hat for the top half. All of this personal equipment fits easily into a single nylon bag. Other back-up gear for more demanding trips would be shared out among the paddlers and could travel in a separate container. This might include: further medical supplies such as an airway, inflatable splints, triangular bandages, wound dressings; stove, fuel, and pot; repair equipment such as canoe tape, sewing kit, epoxy adhesive, footrest bolts; food.

WHAT CAN GO WRONG ON WHITE WATER?

Accidents which occur in white-water kayaking fall into four main categories:
- A paddler takes a swim in a rapid.
- A swimmer becomes held in a stopper.
- The kayak becomes trapped and the paddler is unable to exit.
- Others, of which shoulder dislocation is the most common.

Swimmer in a rapid

The first issue here is that the swimmer must do what he or she can to help. You should use safe rapids with good rescue cover to practise swimming so that you are prepared for it if it ever happens.

To help yourself in rocky, shallow rivers, follow these guidelines:
- Stay upstream of the kayak or push away from it.
- Lie on your back and look downstream.
- Swim to the bank using legs *and* arms.
- Keep hips up and feet up near the surface.

In deep rapids with large waves:
- Stay with the boat for as long as you need to get your strength back.
- Decide upon a bank and swim purposefully and steadily for it.
- Use a front crawl and be determined to get there.

Expert kayakers who rarely leave their kayaks are often the least experienced when it comes to taking an accidental swim. The probability, however, is very high that every kayaker will end up in the water at some stage in his or her life. Be prepared to take a swim by practising, however good you might be *in* the boat.

Do not lie back and wait to be rescued – help yourself.

When you see a rescuer with a throw line:
- Watch the rescuer.
- Spread your arms and legs on the surface to make a larger target.
- Get hold of the rope with both hands.
- Pull it in to your chest and over one shoulder.

Above: Practise swimming in safe white water. Keep your hips and feet up, and look downstream. Always remember to do everything to help yourself.

Below: If you are swimming in a rapid, stay on the upstream side of your kayak and, if you are heading for a drop, swim away from it.

- Float on your back and look at your feet.
- If you roll a little, use your legs in a wide kick to get level again.
- Let yourself swing into the bank.

In a wide, powerful river, the only way you can help a swimmer is to paddle to that person, and try to get him or her ashore using your kayak.

When you spot your swimmer:
- Ferry glide across to the swimmer.
- Aim to make contact behind your hip on the upstream side.
- Get the person on to the rear grab handle.

- After a short rest the swimmer should pull on to the rear deck using the rear deck line.
- Your passenger keeps head down flat and hands on cockpit rim, legs spread wide.
- Paddle to shore.

It is a good idea already to have decided who will rescue the swimmer and who will recover the stray kayak beforehand. The rescuer tows the boat ashore or shunts it by nosing his or her own kayak into the cockpit of the swamped boat. Turn the kayak upright before starting the tow so that it offers less drag.

Above left, above, and left: To receive a line, watch the rescuer and spread your arms and legs. Then, pull the line into your chest (under or over your shoulder). You might submerge for a moment. Stay on your back. Look downstream. Stand up, maintaining your line.

Below: Carrying a swimmer. The swimmer keeps his/her head down, and legs spread widely for stability.

Above: Rescuers with throw-bags should be positioned properly to throw and to land swimmers.

Above: Throwing a line. Open the throw-bag, take out some rope, shout, and signal. Then aim and throw.

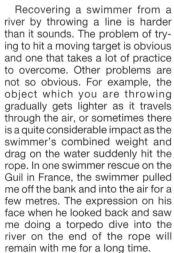

Recovering a swimmer from a river by throwing a line is harder than it sounds. The problem of trying to hit a moving target is obvious and one that takes a lot of practice to overcome. Other problems are not so obvious. For example, the object which you are throwing gradually gets lighter as it travels through the air, or sometimes there is a quite considerable impact as the swimmer's combined weight and drag on the water suddenly hit the rope. In one swimmer rescue on the Guil in France, the swimmer pulled me off the bank and into the air for a few metres. The expression on his face when he looked back and saw me doing a torpedo dive into the river on the end of the rope will remain with me for a long time.

Rescues with the highest degree of certainty are those where a rapid

Above: The rope should lie across the body of the swimmer in the rapid. It takes practice to hit a moving target.

is protected by rescuers positioned *before* the paddlers begin their run. Throw-bags can be prepared and the best positions to throw and land the swimmer can be used. More impromptu rescues are unfortunately quite common; the paddler lands, leaps from the boat, pulls out the throw-bag, and throws it to the swimmer, all in a matter of seconds. It is at such times that training and discipline count most. Stick to these rules when using a throw-bag:
- Open the bag – take out the end plus an arm's length of rope.
- Signal and shout.
- Aim.

Above: Sit down and brace with your feet. It is a good idea to use a shoulder belay, too. It gives you an even more stable position.

- Throw.
- Sit down and brace with your feet.

Aim to overshoot the swimmer slightly so that you lie the rope across him or her. A better way to hold the rope is to use a shoulder belay before you throw. It is, however, still important to sit and brace.

Use a javelin throw if:
- The distance is great (over 15 metres/50 feet).
- You have to throw fast because of wind.
- You find you are more accurate that way.

THE SHOULDER RELAY

SPLITTING THE COILS

USING WATER-FILLED BAGS

Above left: Aim the throw-bag to overshoot the swimmer slightly.

Above: Throw using a javelin throw for longer distances.

You must practise with your throw-bag so that you can make your first throw count.

If you miss the first throw:
- Pull the rope in, making coils as you do it.
- Run along the bank to get ahead of the swimmer.
- Get to a near point or a high spot which will help your throw.
- Split the coils and throw the half with the bag, letting the others pay out.
- Drop the coils and hold the end.
- Fill the bag with water.
- Signal — aim – throw.
- Sit and brace.

All paddlers should carry a personal throw-bag with approximately 15 metres (50 feet) of rope in it. This makes for a neat, easy-to-handle package which is light enough for anyone to carry around. It can be repacked within thirty seconds, so you are not reluctant to run out the rope. On wide rivers, it is good to have a 25-metre (80-foot) bag in the group. The increased single span that this gives you is very important in some rescues but it is a length of rope which takes time and care in handling.

Your personal throw-bag is a piece of equipment with which you should become familiar. Use it often; do not pack it away as some

CARRYING THE THROW-BAG

Stored behind the seat and held in place by the airbag, the throw-bag is easy to reach.

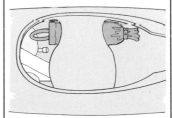

Many kayaks have a space at the side of the seat which will hold a throw-bag perfectly.

Some paddlers carry a throw-bag in a compartment in the buoyancy aid. This kind of availability has much to recommend it but there is considerable restriction to the paddler's movements.

sacred, life-saving device only to be touched in emergencies. Know how it behaves, practise your knots with it, hang your wet gear on it, and do not be frightened of it.

Swimmer in a stopper

Finding a swimmer in a stopper is possibly the worst rescue situation with which you can be confronted. The swimmer is often well out of reach and the risk to the rescuers is high. The powerful tow-back pulls the swimmer into the weir, where he or she is forced under and the current carries the person downstream until he or she surfaces and is drawn into the back-tow again. The aerated water gives little flotation to help keep head above water so the more personal buoyancy the swimmer is wearing the better are the chances of getting a breath.

If you capsize and find yourself held in a back-tow:
● Get hold of your boat – this helps you to get a breath and also marks your position for rescuers.

If help is not forthcoming:
● Swim towards the weir face.
● Let the water tumbling over the weir take you down – a powerful current of downstream moving water will take you away from the surface back-tow.

This is a frightening prospect but, if there is no help, it is the way out and it uses the power of the water to

FLOATING A BOAT ON A LINE

Only a kayak with maximum internal flotation should be used for this. Floating it in from downstream is more difficult but lessens the risk of injuring the swimmer with it. A second rope from the opposite bank can be used to pull the boat into position.

THROW-LINES SPANNING THE RIVER

Initially, rope ends can be thrown across or carried by a paddler. Walk the rope up and drop it in.

A swimmer caught in the back tow of a deep circulating stopper. Holding on to the swimmer's kayak helps him/her to stay on the surface and marks his/her position for rescuers.

your advantage. The commonly heard advice, 'Swim down', is not strictly correct. If you are not close to the weir face you might easily be swimming *against* water *rising* into the back-tow.

It has been suggested that removing the buoyancy aid will help a swimmer to escape from a stopper. This is an action which I would emphatically advise against. As far as I know, there is no known case of someone being drowned through wearing a lifejacket or buoyancy aid.

The additional flotation given is essential if you are to get air before you dive under and, when you surface, it will assist you considerably to recover from the inevitable state of exhaustion.

To rescue someone from a stopper, you should get everyone to work as a team.
• Get a rope to the swimmer.
• Cover the person from downstream in case he or she is washed out. Use a good paddler in a kayak to do this but keep away from the back-tow.

To use the throw-bag:
• Get several bags ready.
• Shout – aim – throw.
• If the swimmer is having trouble seeing the rope, tie a buoyancy aid to the end.

If this simple and quick attempt fails or cannot work, possibly because of too great a distance for the throw-bag, unsuitable bank access, or because the swimmer cannot see the bag being thrown, there are other options.
• Float in a boat on a line. It is easier to push in from upstream but there is obviously some danger to the swimmer.
• Use a kayak with air bags, deck lines, and, if there is time, put the spray cover on and tie it off.

There are many situations where the span of the river would be too great but otherwise using a drag line to span the river is an excellent system. Two throw-bags connected together work well. Additional flotation and visibility can be added with a buoyancy aid clipped on to the throw-bags.

A swimmer caught in the back tow of a stopper. Keeping hold of the kayak makes him visible.

The advantages of using a drag line are that there is: no risk to rescuers; ropes can be positioned accurately; and the swimmer can be pulled to either side of the river. On the other hand, the system takes time to set up and does not work on curved weirs.

If the distance is too far to throw, the bag end of the rope is taken across by a kayaker. The person on the bank feeds it to the kayaker from a high point if possible to try to keep it out of the water.

Another method of rescue involves a kayaker on a rope. A rope is taken through the end grab handle and clipped on to the paddler's chest harness. The advantage of this method is that the kayak can be positioned accurately so that the swimmer can make contact with it but, again, it does take time to set up and there is some risk to the paddler. The kayaker must use a signal to show when he or she wishes to be pulled from the back-tow.

The system using two kayaks should be used only on small stoppers. The upstream kayaker allows the boat to flood in towards the swimmer. The downstream paddler has the rescue kayak on the tow line and helps to hold the kayak straight in the back-tow. Once contact is made with the swimmer, both paddlers reverse away from the weir.

Stopper rescues are not easy to simulate with any degree of safety although, if large polythene drums are used as 'swimmers', you can at least experiment with positioning ropes and crossing the river. It is a good thing to discuss rescue of swimmers when you come across nasty stoppers which you have no intention of paddling. This develops the 'problem-solving' frame of mind, which is so important to have in a real emergency.

Entrapment

Accidents where a kayak becomes pinned on the river bed or on an obstruction are, unfortunately, very common. A very high proportion of these entrapments occur in sections of river which are not in the extreme category of difficulty but in the medium to easy grades. This could initially be accounted for by the greater number of paddlers working at this level but it is also true to say that less experienced kayakers often underestimate the risk and the seriousness of such incidents on what is considered low-graded water.

Paddlers on extreme white-water rapids which pose a high entrapment threat usually cover the rapids with bank support equipped to work quickly to extract the person in the boat. The rescue cover, and often the equipment, are missing on easier-grade rivers, and so it can take a long time to organize and carry out a rescue. The conse-

KAYAKER ON A ROPE	THE BACK-TOW

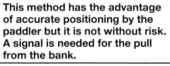

This method has the advantage of accurate positioning by the paddler but it is not without risk. A signal is needed for the pull from the bank.

This method is extremely hazardous to the paddlers. The downstream kayak faces downstream. He watches for the signal to tow out.

quences of this, where a paddler's head is underwater, are obvious.

Some kayaks are predisposed to pinning by nature of their shape and construction. The following characteristics make a kayak more resistant to it and reduce the risk of paddler entrapment:

1 Broad rounded ends – buoyant and less likely to snag.

2 High volume – floats higher and presents softer contours to reduce the grip of the water.

3 Rigid hull material – the hard surface is less likely to 'cup' boulders, etc. It tends to slide off.

4 Maximum internal flotation – if the boat is swamped, it should continue to ride high so that most of the river power continues to pass underneath.

5 Safety cockpit.

The three ways in which a kayak can become pinned are shown in the illustrations.

Vertical pins occur on shallow drops and ledges. Often, the nose of the kayak is snagged in an undetected crevice. Hauling or pushing

the boat upwards, that is, reversing its path in, will sometimes let it clear the obstruction and continue downstream. Water swilling around the kayak holds it down as if glued to the lip of the drop and, if it swamps with water, this effect becomes very pronounced. The pressure of water on the paddler's back often holds the person firmly into the boat. Broaching causes the kayak to flatten and then fold. The cockpit is usually upstream so the swamping occurs very quickly.

If you are involved in rescuing someone in an entrapment, there is a number of important points to remember.

1 Is the paddler able to breathe? The paddler's head might be above the surface or the person could be breathing from a capsule of air formed in front of the face even though the head appears to be underwater. If the paddler cannot breathe try to get his or her head above water but, if you cannot do this, start trying to move the boat.

2 Stabilize the kayak and the pad-

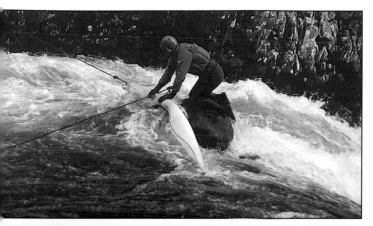

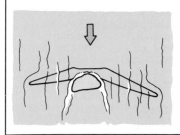

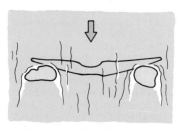

dler so that it does not sink further or roll over. A rope around the paddler's chest and under the arms could be used in a vertical pin.

3 Free the paddler. Make a quick plan. Cut the paddler free and/or work on freeing the kayak. If the paddler is breathing you have a bit more time to decide on a good plan.

If the paddler cannot help himself or herself to get out, it will be extremely difficult physically to drag the person out. Hands and arms are slippery, and clothing tends to pull off. If the paddler is wearing a chest harness, clipping into the rear of this is the best bet. Breaking or cutting the kayak in front of the cockpit makes it much easier for the paddler to get out. A polyethylene kayak will need to be cut with a saw.

Once you have secured a rope to the grab handle, consider the angle at which you will pull to free the boat

---

Above left: A swamped kayak with airbags in addition to the standard foam-wall flotation. In the test, the boat has to be tied in position to keep it on the rock.

Left: Without airbags, the same kayak becomes submerged and 'glued' against the rock.

Far left: A break-away cockpit area. This is another system which makes escape easier.

Left: Another system which has been devised to reduce the danger of entrapment. The cockpit and deck area breaks away when the rim is pushed forward. This was developed in the United States for kayaks constructed from fibreglass.

KAYAK PINNING

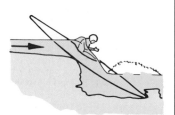

VERTICAL PIN

A rope positioned under the paddler's arms can help, but be careful not to catch his or her neck.

HORIZONTAL AND VERTICAL PULL

The kayak is hoisted from the grip of the current on the upward rope and, when freed, is swung in on the low rope.

VECTOR PULL

A superb system. Tie off the rope taut and then pull at right-angles to it in the middle. Clip on another rope if necessary.

Right: Directing the pull upwards by running the hauling rope through a sling and karabiner positioned high on a tree.

Below: Lowering a rescuer into an entrapment on a bridge pier. He can attach a hauling rope, lift the victim's head, and possibly even cut the boat to free the legs. The victim and rescuer are raised using a pulley hoist. This needs a lot of rope.

most easily. Often, in a side-on pin, pulling across the current is the only practical choice, but if a vertical hoist can be rigged quickly, it can remove most of the kayak from the grip of the current. This kind of hoist works ideally where a paddler is trapped on a bridge pier. A rescuer is lowered on to the kayak to raise the paddler's head and clip the grab handle. The freed paddler can be hauled on a separate rope.

If you are faced with the enormous pressure that any river can exert on a pinned kayak, you must take every advantage possible, especially when working alone. Forces of 400 kilograms (900 pounds) have been measured when pinned kayaks have been hauled. With a turn of the rope around your body, good footwear, and traction, you can exert about 120 per cent of your body weight as a straight pull on to a rope. Pulling at right angles to a taut, tied-off rope is an excellent way to gain mechanical advantage. It also leaves the kayak tethered if it suddenly swings free.

Rigging a pulley hoist is another way of increasing the pull on a rope. Two karabiners and a secure anchorage are required.

Freeing a trapped kayak using a vector pull.

RIGGING A PULLEY HOIST

Tie on to the trapped kayak. Attach a sling or end of rope to a strong anchorage (tree) and clip a karabiner into it.

Clip the rope back into the karabiner at the tree.

Tie a slip knot in the rope and clip in another karabiner.

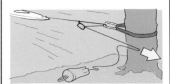

Clip the haul rope into this and pull.

This gives a threefold increase in your pulling power. A single person of average body weight can exert about 170 kilograms (560 pounds) using this system. Some energy is lost to friction on the karabiners. This can be reduced dramatically by running the rope through light-weight caving pulleys.

RESCUE ORGANIZATION

If you are working alone on a rescue, your own safety is of paramount importance because without you to guide in further help (if it comes to this), the rescue becomes a search which could take days. If other paddlers are available, it might be possible to run several rescue attempts at the same time. Provided you do not get in each other's way, this is a good plan, particularly in a very urgent situation. An example of this would be a vertical pin. One group should make contact with the paddler and try to get the person to free himself or herself while another sets up a hoist to lift the boat.

Whatever the accident and however urgent are the circumstances always:
1 Think first.
2 Then act.

SHOULDER DISLOCATION

This is a relatively common accident in white-water kayaking. It usually occurs when a paddler is bracing across a hole or stopper and is suddenly capsized. The paddle hitting the river bed, or even the force of the capsize, transmits a shock to the arm which shoots the head of the upper arm bone forwards and out of the shallow cup which forms part of the shoulder joint.

The anterior dislocation is usually very painful and prevents further paddling. The paddler should support the arm, slightly away from the body in a characteristic position. The first-aid treatment is to help to immobilize the arm with a sling followed by a wrapping to prevent outward movement. The arm should be 'padded' into the position of comfort before the wrapping is applied. Relocating the shoulder should be left to a doctor unless you are in remote country. In this case you should get medical training for this kind of problem before you go.

SHOULDER DISLOCATION

This kind of brace can result in dislocation of the lower arm. Keep the lower arm bent and in front of the body line.

SPECIALIZED RESCUE EQUIPMENT

Chest harness

The chest harness makes it possible for a rescuer to be held safely on a rope in the current. It also provides a grab handle for rescuers trying to get hold of the person to be rescued. There are two types:

1 Separate harness.

2 Integral harness and buoyancy aid.

The separate harness is inter-changeable between paddlers without removing the buoyancy aid. This is its only advantage. The integral system is much more stable and comfortable and also helps to mould the buoyancy aid to the trunk, making it warmer and more secure.

A rope is attached to the harness at a mid-point between the base of the shoulder blades. When you are held by a rope against the current from this suspension point, you are on your back with arms and legs streaming. Even in very strong currents, this is quite practical as water fountains around and over your head, leaving your face in air. The harness is fitted with a buckle which

Above: This buoyancy aid has an integral chest harness with quick release.

Above: The integral chest harness buoyancy aid. The rope clips into the strap at the rear.

will release with a single action and allow the swimmer to float free from the rope.

The chest harness should be used in *any* situation where it is necessary to attach yourself to a rope in the river, and it is also used

Below: A rescuer held on a chest harness in increasing strengths of current. Keep looking downstream so that the face stays in air. With this equipment, a rescuer can more safely enter the river to retrieve boats.

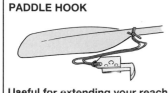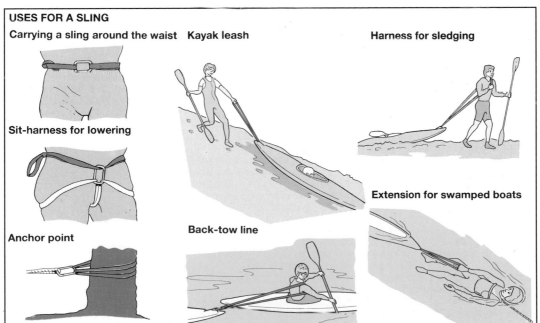
to anchor a bank-based rescuer so that he or she can hold a load on a rope without being dragged into the river.

Towing systems

Towing from a kayak has no place on narrow, shallow rivers. The numerous boulders showing through and tight bends offer too many snag points to the tow line. In a wide river, towing can easily be the only fast and positive way of getting swamped kayaks and, in some cases, swamped paddlers ashore. No towing system is entirely safe and any towing activity should be confined to long, flat runs-out at the end of a rapid.

The kayaker can choose one of two points of attachment from which to tow: the body or the boat. Body-tow systems fit around the waist and have a quick-release mechanism on the front. This works well on flat water giving a conveniently adjustable length of tow rope. It is unsuitable for white water because of the risk of entanglement and of applying pressure directly to the paddler's body. Because the equipment is largely non-life-saving in its nature, this risk is not justifiable. It is always possible that the paddler might not be able to operate the quick-release mechanism.

Kayak-mounted tow systems are anchored, usually to the rear of the cockpit by a quick-release mechanism. The tow line is either taken through a loop at the rear or is run directly from the towing anchorage. It should be possible to operate any attachment to a kayak with cold hands. Don't forget to turn towed kayaks upright to reduce drag.

Paddle hook

This simple tool turns the kayak paddle into a useful rescue aid especially for entrapments. It extends your reach by 2 metres (6.5 feet) making it possible to attach a rope in circumstances which might otherwise be impossible. Several models of paddle hook exist. My own preference is for the small, neat one which clamps to the edge of the blade. Peter Reithmaier of Austria has also developed a simple, light-weight clamp which joins paddles to give an even greater reach.

The facility for extending your reach has many applications in river rescue. This specialist gear must however, be simple and quick to use.

Sling

The sling is a loop of tape used in rock climbing. It is usually made

USES FOR A SLING

Carrying a sling around the waist   Kayak leash

Harness for sledging

Sit-harness for lowering

Extension for swamped boats

Anchor point

Back-tow line

from a 2.4-metre (8-foot) length of nylon tape sewn at the joint. In white water, the sling has many uses both in rescue and for more general application. It is the quickest way to anchor off the end of a rope for a handline or for setting up a hoist. A handy way to carry the sling is shortened with an overhand knot and joined by a karabiner around the waist. Climbing slings are extremely strong but sink if you drop them. Polypropylene webbing is weaker but floats. Both sink beautifully if ballasted by the weight of a karabiner. Being aware of this is really all that is needed.

Pulleys

Pulleys lower the friction of ropes pressing through karabiners in a hoist. They are small, light, strong, and require virtually no maintenance. There are many river trips where you are never going to need to rig a powerful hoist. On rivers where entrapment is likely they are well worth considering.

Saw

A small, folding pruning saw will cut fibreglass or polyethylene reasonably easily. Its teeth are of the 'ripsaw' nature which means that they cut on both push and pull strokes. If you can get both hands on the job, you can make a 45-centimetre (18-inch) lengthwise cut away from the cockpit in about thirty seconds. Kayaks with foam walls in the foredeck are easy to cut alongside the wall.

PROCEDURE ON THE RIVER

Leadership

Good leadership is a fundamental part of safety on white water. Even a group of paddlers of equal expertise operate more efficiently and safely if they are co-ordinated by a leader. The leader does not necessarily lay down the law all the time. He or she also behaves as a chairperson to summarize the views of everyone in the party, to be aware of the weak and the strong paddlers, and to bring common sense to bear in those all-too frequent moments of mass indecision. The leader may also be required physically to lead

on rapids. This is no easy task for the leader must choose a route and move at a speed that makes him/her visible to paddlers behind and avoid the tempting little eddies which would hold only his or her own kayak, possibly leaving an inexperienced paddler to cope alone. Large numbers of paddlers create problems for one another on white water, so it is safer to work in smaller teams of three or four. Paddlers working in small groups identify more readily with their responsibility towards each other. They learn to share taking the lead on rapids as well as the importance of checking constantly on each other and meeting up in larger eddies.

The end paddler

The last paddler in any group should be a very mature kayaker. He or she is the person most commonly out of sight of the others and if the end paddler ever gets into trouble, there will be the greatest time lag before help arrives. This person must be equipped to deal with rescue of all kinds and skilful enough to use what eddies are left when he/she finds the group sitting waiting.

Hand signals

Communication between paddlers is often difficult because of the distance which must be preserved between kayaks and also because of the noise of white water. Basic information has to be passed between paddlers by signals which they have agreed beforehand. What you signal must be information concerning safety only and the number of signals must be kept very small. What you use must be readable from behind as well as from the front because the leading paddler might want to signal without having to turn around.

● *Use* the system so that it becomes familiar to you before you get into difficult water and you are obliged to signal.
● Make sure that it is known and used by bank support.
● Relay the signal through the group.
● If in doubt pull in and get out.

Bank support

The bank support consists of any organization set up to give safety cover on a rapid. It could consist of a single paddling partner or it might be a team of people whose only role is to give rescue cover and support.

To give useful rescue cover, the individuals involved must either have the kayaking experience to set up in the right positions with appropriate equipment or be thoroughly briefed on the following:
● What the main hazards are.
● What the likely trouble spots will be and the consequences of a paddler being involved in them.
● What to do in this event.
● What equipment they should use and how to secure themselves.
● The overall distribution of cover throughout the rapid complex.

The bank support should control the signalling to paddlers waiting to run the rapid. Every member of the support team should be equipped with: a helmet; buoyancy aid; throwbag and karabiner; knife. If they are to be used for wading or swimming, they must have a wetsuit or drysuit. Fellow paddlers make excellent support teams because they understand the dangers, are well equipped, and have natural anticipation of problems.

'WHAT IF?'

The key to safety lies within the paddler's ability to bring past experience to bear on the unknown nature of the time ahead. You must learn to anticipate problems by asking, 'What if?' If you are a leader, you

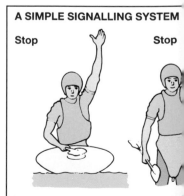

A SIMPLE SIGNALLING SYSTEM

Stop   Stop

A well-equipped bank-support team working on a vertically pinned kayak.

SOLOING

If you paddle alone, you are taking the greatest risk possible in white-water kayaking and, if you are considering a solo journey, you should examine your motives closely. One of the main advantages of moving alone in other outdoor sports, such as mountaineering and rock climbing, is that you can move faster, without the hindrance of rope lengths or the distraction of another person. Soloing is unlikely to give an overall increase in speed of movement to the white-water paddler; in fact, the need to do all the reconnaissance work alone will make progress slower and take a greater toll on energy.

The benefits are essentially 'spiritual'; heightening of concentration; increasing awareness of the whole surroundings, and the satisfaction of total self-reliance. Soloing well within your limits remains very risky and is indefensible on grounds of safety but it is considered by some paddlers to be a very special white-water experience.

DEALING WITH DROWNING

Each of us has a duty to know what to do if confronted with a drowning kayaker. As in the case of all rescue procedure, you must be entirely honest with yourself and ask the question, 'Would I really know what to do?' When you ask that question, you have taken the first step.

The basic circulation
Oxygen is required for the tissues of

must be expert at this before you take anyone on to white water. You will be constantly playing over incidents and rescues in your mind especially when inspecting rapids. Your equipment and your pacing on the river will reflect this anticipation.

Good leaders on white water quite naturally find that this instinct for trouble extends into their own paddling, subconsciously limiting its scope. Many would argue that this is a good thing and not to be interfered with while some say that if you are committed to pushing limits you must free your mind from all inhibiting influences. One thing is certain – ignoring the danger does not make it go away.

Carry on   Go that way   Something nasty ahead

our bodies to remain alive. By breathing, we maintain a flow of oxygen-rich air into and out of our lungs. Inside the lungs is a mass of tiny blood vessels which cause the circulating blood to take on some of this oxygen. As you know, the heart provides the pumping energy, working on two circuits. One circuit pushes blood out of the heart into the oxygenating lungs and back to the heart. The second circuit takes this blood and carries it into the general body circulation to distribute the oxygen. The brain, of course, is part of the general circulation but it is extremely sensitive to a reduction or cessation of oxygen supply.

Drowning

Drowning causes this supply of oxygen to be shut off and can start seriously to damage the brain within four to five minutes. The process of breathing is controlled by the brain and so this ceases to work. Because the heart is not controlled directly by the brain, it can continue to beat although eventually it, too, will fail as a result of the lack of oxygen.

In the early stages of drowning, the person usually draws water deeply into the throat. This triggers off a reflex, called a laryngo-spasm, in the muscles at the top of the windpipe. The reflex prevents water from entering the windpipe but also causes asphyxiation and results in unconsciousness. This is sometimes referred to as 'dry drowning'. Wet drowning, where the lungs are found to have taken in water, is less common and is a result of failure or relaxation of the laryngo-spasm.

COLD

Sudden immersion in cold water can be the cause of another automatic response of the body. This is a reflex which drastically reduces circulation of blood and slows heart rate so that the body lives on a tiny fraction of its normal oxygen requirement. The pulse is hard to find and breathing is very shallow, making it hard to detect signs of life. Victims in this extreme survival state have been revived after being submerged for as long as thirty-eight

minutes. The reflex does not always occur but you should be aware of it to give you hope in your persistence with what is called cardio-pulmonary resuscitation (*see* below). If you are faced with an unconscious person, you should take the following action:
● **Check for breathing**
feel for air movement on your lips or cheeks;
a person who is not breathing has a blue-grey colour of skin and lips.
● **If there is no breathing**
start resuscitation immediately.
● **Check for pulse**
place two fingers to the side of the adam's apple and feel for pulse.
● **If there is no pulse**
start cardio-pulmonary resuscitation (CPR).

Resuscitation and cardio-pulmonary resuscitation

Remember the following vital 'a, b, c':
● Clear the **a**irway.
● Check the **b**reathing and resuscitate if necessary.
● Check the **c**irculation and give cardiac compression if required.

Any obstruction of the air through mouth, throat, or windpipe will prevent resuscitation.
● Remove the helmet chinstrap.
● Free any tight collar on the cag etc.
● Remove any vomit from the mouth with your fingers.

Knowledge of resuscitation saved the life of this paddler. His helmet has been removed and he has been placed in the coma or recovery position.

● Tilt the head backwards and apply lift to the jaw.
This action is often enough to allow breathing to begin spontaneously. If it does not, then you will need to begin resuscitation.
● Tilt the head to clear the airway as before.
● Pinch the casualty's nose to seal it.
● Make a good mouth-to-mouth seal.
● Give four quick breaths without a pause.
● Watch for the chest rising in response to inflation.
● Remove the seal – the chest should sink.
● Check pulse – feel for 10 to 15 seconds.
If there is a pulse, continue inflation at a rate of one every five seconds. If there is no pulse, you must begin cardio-pulmonary resuscitation.
● Get the casualty on to a firm surface.
● Remove the buoyancy aid.
● Feel for the bottom of the breast bone at the 'apex' of the ribs and measure two finger widths up from it towards the head.
● Place the heel of the other hand

beside the fingers and then cover that hand with the heel of the first hand.

- Rock forwards with straight arms and compress the breast bone by 4 to 5 centimetres (1½ to 2 inches) for about a half-second.
- Relax – half-second – repeat.
- Fifteen compressions.
- Two breaths.
- Repeat.
- Check the pulse after one minute.
- If you have help, one person should carry out resuscitation, while the other does compressions at the rate of five compressions to one breath.
- With children, apply lighter compressions and smaller inflations.

The casualty recovers pulse first, then breathing, and finally consciousness. Remember, that as the casualty regains consciousness, the predrowning struggle often starts up again and the person should be secured if perched on a narrow ledge. Place him or her in the recovery position and protect the casualty from cold. Stay beside the person's head to check breathing and pulse. If the casualty does not revive, you should continue CPR until medical help arrives.

With a non-breathing casualty, you should make the first inflation as soon as possible. The rate of inflations is much less critical. In one case, a paddler picked up an unconscious swimmer at the end of a rapid and managed to give a few inflations while paddling to the bank. The rescue was successful. In a rescue in which I was involved, a non-breathing casualty revived when his helmet chinstrap was released and his head tilted backwards.

Any person who has been revived from drowning must be hospitalized because there are several serious conditions which can develop afterwards.

TRAINING AND PRACTICE

You should obtain expert tuition in CPR and practise regularly using a training manikin. Include swimming with a casualty in your rescue practice so that you can appreciate the difficulty of working alone with an unconscious person.

HYPOTHERMIA

The body functions by maintaining a heat balance. You produce heat when you exercise; you 'tick over' at a basic level when you sit still; and you use clothing to prevent heat loss to the surroundings. When you start to feel cold, you can exercise to produce *more* heat or add clothing to *preserve* the present level. It is easy to see why the white water kayaker is so vulnerable because supplies of both energy to manufacture heat and clothing to save it are limited. The water in which the paddler is likely to be immersed, particularly when taking a swim, is often very cold and capable of removing body heat extremely quickly.

Whichever the means by which heat is lost, such as immersion, wind chill, or exhaustion, if the heat taken away is greater than the heat produced and retained, you will become **hypothermic**. It is the beginning of a dangerous spiral which can have a disastrous end.

The aim should be to prevent hypothermia by wearing good, insulating kayak clothing and to choose rivers which you know you can handle. Recognize it in yourself and in others in its early stages and hypothermia is simple to treat. Allow it to develop and you are asking for problems which will soon be well beyond your control.

Mild hypothermia
- You feel intensely cold and start shivering.
- Your face is white because the circulation to the surface of the skin has started to shut down.
- If you get colder you will find your co-ordination of fine movements is lost and balance is affected.

At this stage you must prevent any further heat loss. This means you must put on more clothing, and stay out of the water and out of the chilling effect of the wind. Exercising will help produce more heat naturally. A person who is allowed to cool beyond this stage reaches a point where the body cannot rewarm itself through exercise. The

body core temperature sinks to 32-35° (90-95°F) and it is virtually impossible to stand. Shivering ceases, muscles become rigid, and speech is practically impossible. The treatment is to provide warm insulation in a warm atmosphere – not easy in the field. Body heat from other paddlers can be used by surrounding the casualty. There is no clear distinction between the stages in mild hypothermia. The deeper a person sinks into the condition, the more you have to create and maintain body heat for him or her to rewarm the body.

- Get the casualty into a bivouac shelter with other people.
- Insulate the person from the ground.
- The casualty will be tucked in a ball. Wrap yourself around the casualty from behind. Use another person to lie against his or her front.
- Cover with warm insulation – sleeping bags, warm jackets.
- Keep air movement to a minimum so that your breath warms the space inside the shelter.
- Get a stove going or light a fire so that warm air is trapped around you.
- Reassure the casualty.
- Pre-warm insulation and pack it around him.

Profound hypothermia
In this stage the casualty is unconscious. The action of insulating and sheltering should be continued but there must be the absolute minimum of movement. The profoundly hypothermic casualty has receded into what is sometimes called a 'metabolic icebox'. This is a survival mechanism which is geared to a body functioning at a low temperature. There is little sign of life. The greatest danger is that of the heart going into fibrillation which is an ineffective beating rhythm. Sudden movement of the casualty, rapid rewarming, or even sitting the person upright are each enough to trigger fibrillation. Speed of evacuation is no longer the priority. Careful, gentle movement is much more important. Even in hospital the casualty can have little done for him except to be given intravenous fluid to maintain the blood volume. This situation should be avoided.

CHAPTER 8

COMPETITIVE WHITE-WATER KAYAKING

Competitive kayaking on white water takes the form of racing against the clock. Like ski racing, there are two separate disciplines, one being a straight, timed run, and the other being a test of manoeuvrability through gates.

WILD-WATER RACING

A competitor in a wild-water race comes to the start line alone. Ahead lies a stretch of river which will be of Grade III standard of difficulty or more. Although the course will be 3 kilometres (1.9 miles) minimum distance, the paddler will have a clear image of every piece of it in his or her mind. The aim is to paddle it as fast as possible and to turn in a finish time which beats the paddlers who have been sent off ahead as well as those who are still to go.

The paddler's speed over the course is not determined just by level of fitness, although this plays a major part. The competitor must understand completely the movement of water through boulder fields, around bends, and over drops and he or she must use this knowledge to devise a route through the rapids which will give pure, uninterrupted speed. The choice of route for the various sections of rapids will have been made

Top right: World Championships white-water racing on the River Isére in the French Alps.

Bottom right: A racer in the middle of a Grade 4 section of rapid. Staying on line is vital or the kayak will be slowed dramatically by eddies and holes.

Far right: The white-water racing kayak is a fast, straight-running machine. It must also have volume to prevent it from plunging deeply into the rough water.

while walking the bank before the race for, when the starter counts down from 5 seconds to Go, every stroke must take the kayak towards the finish without hesitation. During the race, the paddler's 'mental map' of the course unfolds with the route superimposed on to it, taking advantage of jets of fast flow, clipping the sides of standing waves, and avoiding eddies and returning water which might act as a drag on the boat's speed.

With the combined velocity of the water and the paddler pushing the kayak on at full flight, things happen fast. It takes an extremely alert and fit athlete to keep going for the twenty minutes or so to the finish. Experience, training, and guidance from a coach will help you to pace your delivery of energy to the boat throughout the race so that you do not 'blow up' half way down the course or arrive at the finish with too much left.

Equipment

The wild-water racing kayak is designed and tuned purely to give forward directional speed downriver. It does not respond instantly to steering strokes and the paddler's route choice should not involve tight turns anyway because these would have a dramatic braking affect on the boat's speed. The paddler plots the line like a racing driver on a circuit, keeping turns wide and 'straightened out' so that the power can be kept on throughout. To instigate a turn leftwards, say, the kayak is tilted on to its right side. The boat runs to the left. More tilt gives more turn. To the rear of the cockpit are the widest points of the kayak (sometimes called 'the wings'). When tilt is applied in a turn, a wing comes close to or touches the water giving the paddler a little extra stability as he or she tries to keep powering forwards sitting partially on one buttock.

You will notice that the racing kayak has little rocker and that it is extremely buoyant. This, combined with the deep, almost square bow gives the boat superb penetration in rough water so that, seen from the side, it is constantly climbing on to the surface clear of the dragging effect of waves on its decks. The imprint which a wild-water racer's hull leaves on flat water tells us that it is quite a tippy boat to sit in. The waterline shape is long and narrow unless, of course, it is tilted. Being able to sit a racing kayak comfortably takes time. There is no short cut to just clocking up distance on the water. The control of steering by tilting will come quite naturally.

The dimensions and weight of the boat are governed by strict rules. The specifications are:
● Maximum length 4.5 metres (14 feet 9½ inches).
● Minimum width 0.6 metre (1 foot 11½ inches).

• Minimum weight 10 kilograms (22 pounds).

Paddlers in racing are required by the rules to wear a helmet and a buoyancy aid of 6 kilograms (13 pounds 3 ounces) minimum flotation. The kayak must contain flotation and have grab handles at both ends. The paddles used in wild-water racing have asymmetric blades which are spooned in cross-section. These two features give the paddler a much more balanced pull on the shaft and also help the blade to 'lock' into the water very positively. The paddle shaft is slightly shorter than would be used by a flat-water racer and consequently gives the 'high-revving' appearance which is characteristic of wild-water racers. The purpose of this is to keep the boat evenly at its cruising speed with fast, continuous pulls on the blades rather than giving the surges which occur with a longer stroke. This fast rate of paddling also aids the paddler's stability and improves balance while tilting to steer.

Organization

Racing is administered within the National Federations and usually is based on a ranking system with men and women competing separately. There are classes for Canadian singles and doubles as well as kayaks at most events and also a team race for paddlers in threes. Racing takes place at all levels from novice to world championships.

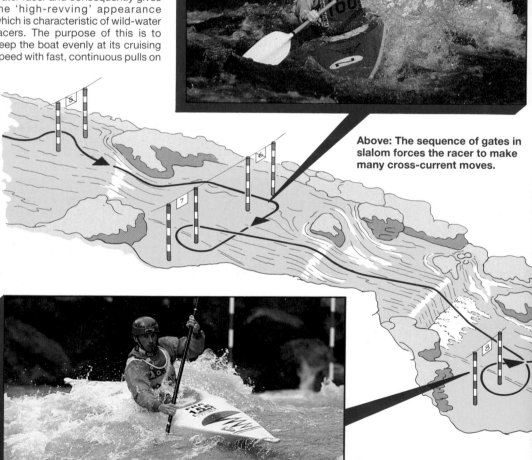

Above: The sequence of gates in slalom forces the racer to make many cross-current moves.

Left: A French competitor lines up on his approach to a break-out. He has the pole and the eddy line clearly in sight.

SLALOM

Like the wild-water racer, the slalom paddler races alone against the clock from the start to the finish line. The problem this time is to pass through approximately twenty-five gates hung above the water, avoiding a touch with any part of the boat, paddle, or body. Each gate is numbered and must be taken sequentially. If you touch a pole, miss a gate, or deliberately push it around your body you are penalized in seconds added to your overall time for the course. Gates are watched by judges who award a clear or penalty score on your entry card for each gate. As well as having to pad-dle the gates in numerical order, you must also pass through them in a designated direction. This direction is indicated by the gate's colour. A gate made up of two red and white poles must be negotiated in an upstream direction. Two green and white poles mean that the gate must be negotiated in a downstream direction. This is worth getting right because the penalty for attempting a gate from the wrong side is fifty seconds! If you are unfortunate enough to capsize and fail to roll up you will be disqualified.

The course designers' job is to hang the gates in such a way as to force the paddler to work out the possible route choices and then to pick the one which will give the best chance to do a fast, clean run. This kind of planning is done from the bank first and then in the boat during the period set aside by the organizers for practice. Each competitor gets two runs on the course and the run which has the better score is automatically taken as the final result.

Despite the intensely competitive nature of slalom, the large gathering of paddlers at events makes for an outstanding social atmosphere. The work on the water is very hard but comes in relatively short bursts and there is lots of time for watching other paddlers and discussing performance. The nature of slalom competition makes it a raw test of boat handling and personal fitness. To paddle a course at full speed and negotiate the gates clearly demands extremely accurate boat control and stroke timing. You must be completely familiar with your kayak and how it will respond to different water formations. No sport could be a more logical extension to pure white-water paddling.

The kayak

The slalom racing kayak is a highly specialized machine. Its decks are almost flat allowing the whole boat to sit low on the surface of the water and permitting it to slip undetected under the hanging poles. The kayak's ends are drawn to fine, chiselled points. This gives two advantages: it offers less 'end' to be dragged across or through the water; the volume of buoyancy in the rear is reduced so that it can be sunk easily into the water to give a pivot turn.

The small space inside a slalom kayak and the extremely light materials from which it is built give an excellent feel. The cockpit is a snug fit and the boat responds to the slightest touch of the paddle. This is undoubtedly the main explanation for the popularity of this type of kayak with young beginners.
Boat specifications:
Minimum length 4 metres (13 feet 2 inches).
Minimum width 0.6 metre (1 foot 11½ inches).

Above: A Swiss racer in a World Championship event. The head and trunk face downstream before the kayak has finished the turn.

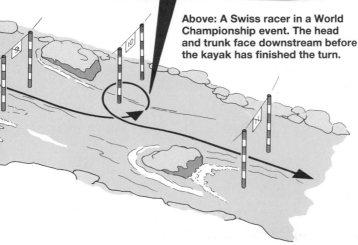

Organization

Once again, a divisional ranking system is usually operated by the National Federations. This provides incentive for paddlers to improve and work their way up through the ranks, and forces the top competitors to work hard to hold their places.

Classes in slalom competitions are:
K1M – Single kayak Men
K1L – Single kayak Ladies
C1 – Single Canadian
C2 – Double Canadian

There is also a team event which comprises three boats, all of which must cross the team gate and the finish line each within fifteen seconds. Events are held at novice level through to World Championships.

Safety

Safey regulations in slalom are strict. All competitors must wear a helmet and personal buoyancy of no less than 6 kilograms (13 pounds 2 ounces) flotation.

At the end of your run, you are required to stay in your boat until the following competitor has finished safely, in case there is a need to give assistance.

Below: A slalom racer between the poles of a gate. There has been a recent change in the colours of the poles used in competition.

Right: The artificial slalom course developed for Holme Pierrepo on the River Trent at Nottingham, England.

Below right: The slalom racing kayak is extremely low in volume, allowing it to squeeze its decks below the poles.

INTERNATIONAL CANOE FEDERATIONS

ARGENTINA
Federacion Argentina de Conoas
Ave Pte Roque Saenz Pena 615,
9o, Officina 905, 1393 Buenos
Aires, Argentina.
Telephone: 010-541 458-787
Telex: 17499 Coarg-ar

AUSTRALIA
Australian Canoe Federation
Room 510, Sports House, 157,
Gloucester Street, Sydney, N.S.W.
2000, Australia.

AUSTRIA
Osterreichischer Kanu Verband
Berggasse 16, 1090 Wien, Austria.
Telephone: 010-43-222 249-203
Telex: 133 132 Sport A

BELGIUM
Royal Belgian Canoe Federation
Geerdegmvaart 79, 2800
Mechelen, Belgium.
Telephone: 010-32-15 415-495

BRAZIL
Carioca Canoeing Association
Ave. Grande Canal 285, Barra de
Tijuca,
Rio de Janeiro, Brazil.

BRITAIN
British Canoe Union
Flexel House, High Street,
Addlestone,
Weybridge, KT15 1JV

BULGARIA
Bulgarian Canoe Federation
Bulevar Tolbuhina 18, Sofia,
Bulgaria.
Telephone: 010-3592-86-51
(333,234)
Telex: 22723 or 22724 BSFS

CANADA
Canadian Canoe Association
333 River Road, Vanier City,
Ontario, K1L 8B9, Canada.
Telephone: 0101-613-74-65-455
Telex: 053-3660

CHILE
Federacion Chilena de Canotaje,
Compania 2982, Casilla 154,
Santiago, Chile.

CHINA
Chinese Canoe Association
9, Tiyukuan Road, Peking,
Peoples Republic of China.
Telephone: 75-13-13.
Telex: 22323 Choc Cn

COSTA RICA
Costa Rica Canoe Federation
Apartado 472-1200, Pavas, Costa
Rica.

CUBA
Federacion Cubana de Canotaje
Via Blanca y Boyeros Suidad
Deportiva,
La Habana, Cuba.
Telephone: 010-53-7 405-805

CYPRUS
Cyprus Canoe Association
P.O. Box 4222, Nicosia, Cyprus.
Telephone: 010-357-21-430-96 (7)

CZECHOSLOVAKIA
Ceskoslovensky Svaz Kanoistiky
Na Porici 12, 11530 Praha 1, CSSR.
Telephone: 010-42-2-249-841
Telex: 122650 SCTV (Canoe)

DENMARK
Dans Kano of Kajak Forbund
Idraettens Hus, Brondby Stadium
20,
DK-2605 Brandby, Denmark.
Telephone: 010-45-2-455555
Telex: 33 111 IDRAET DK

FINLAND
Suomen Kancottiliitto ry
Radiokatu 12, 00240 Helsinki 25,
Finland.
Telephone: 010-358-0 158-23-63
Telex: 121797 Svul SF

FRANCE
Federation Francaise de Canoe
Kayak
17 Route de Vienne, 69007 Lyon,
France.
Telephone: 010-33-78-61-28-06

GERMANY
Deutscher Kanu-Verband
Berta-Allee 8, 4100 Duisberg 1,
Federal Republic of Germany.
Telephone: 010-49-203-72-965 (6)
Telex: 203 389 Kanu

**GERMAN DEMOCRATIC
REPUBLIC**
Deutscher Kanu-Sport-Verband
der DDR
Storkower Strasse 118, 1055 Berlin,
German Democratic Republic.
Telephone: (37-2) 43-84-342
Telex: 114919 DTSB

GREECE
Athletic Club of Neo Petritsi
(Canoa)
24, Mikilon Steet, 24, 54643
Thessaloniki, Greece.

HOLLAND
Nederlandse Kano Bond
Utrechtseweg 17, Postbus 434,
1380, Ak Weesp, Netherlands.
Telephone: 010-31-2940-18-331

HONG KONG
Hong Kong Canoe Union
Queen Elizabeth Stadium, Room
1010,
18 Oi Kwan Rd, Wan Chai, Hong
Kong.
Telephone: 010-852-5-72-70-08
Telex: 65188 HCH HX

HUNGARY
Magyar Kajak-Kenu Szovetseg
Dozsa Gyorgy Ut 1-3, 1143
Budapest, Hungary.
Telephone: 010-36-1-136-427
Telex: 225101 OTSH H

INDIA
Indian Kayaking and Canoeing
Association
606 Akash Deep, 6th Floor,
Barakhambra Road, New Delhi,
India.
Telephone: 010-91-11-331-27-73
Telex: 31-3629 AMBT IN

INDONESIA
Indonesian Canoe Association
Jalan Prapatan 38, Jakarta 10410,
Indonesia.
Telephone: 010-62-21-34-86-85
Telex: 45214 Koni Ia

IRAN
Canoe-Kajak & Water Ski
Federation
10, Avenue Varzandeh, Mejab,
Teheren-Amjadieh, Islamic
Republic of Iran.
Telephone: 010-98-21-225-196
Telex: 212696 Varz Ir

IRELAND
Irish Canoe Union
4/5 Eustace Street, Dublin 2, Eire.
Telephone: 0001-71-43-11

ISRAEL
4, Marmorek Street, PO Box 4575,
6104 Tel Aviv, Israel
Telephone: 010-972-3-24-31-68
Telex: 5786

ITALY
Federazione Italiana Canoe Kajak
Viale Tiziano 70, 00196 Roma, Italy
Telephone: 010-39-6390-954
Telex: 000450 OONI (Oanoa)

IVORY COAST
Federation Ivorienne de Pirogue
OI.B.P. 4733, Abidjan, Ivory Coast.
Telephone: 010-223-331-708

JAPAN
Japan Canoe Federation
Kishi Memorial, 1-1-1 Jinnan,
Shibuya-ku, Tokyo, Japan.
Telephone. 010-81-3-481-2400
Telex: 27697 J

KOREA (North)
Canoe Association of the DDR
Korea, Munsin-Dong 2,
Dongdawon District,
Pyongyang, DPR of Korea.
Telephone: (   ) 62-386
Telex: 5472 KP

KOREA (South)
Korean Canoe Federation
19, Mookyodong, Jung-gu,
Kassa Building Room 605, Seoul
100, Korea.
Telephone: 010-82-2-754-22-40
Telex: 24989 KOCSEL k

LUXEMBOURG
Federation Luxemburgeoise de
Canoe-Kayak
6 Rue de Pulvermuhle, 2356
Luxembourg.
Telex: 3556 Cosl Lu

MALAYSIA
Malaysia Canoe Association
13, Jalan Bungah Orchid,
Hillside Tanjong Bungah, Penang,
Malaysia.

MALTA
Canoeing Association of Malta
Dipartiment ta'l – Edukazzjoni

Lascaris,
Valletta, Malta.
Telephone: 010-356-60-53-92
Telex: 1260 MW

MEXICO
Federacion Mexicana de Canotaje
Xola 1301 -41, Mexico City 03020
DF, Mexico.
Telephone: 010-52-5-530-09-79

NEW ZEALAND
New Zealand Canoeing
Association Inc.
P.O. Box 3768, Wellington, New
Zealand.

NORWAY
Norges Kajak – og Kanoforbund
Hauger Skolovei 1, 1351 Rud,
Norway.
Telephone: 010-47-2-134-290
Telex: 18586 NIF N

PANAMA
Union Panamena de Canotaje,
Apartado 2927, Panolimpic,
Panama 3,
Republic of Panama.

POLAND
Polski Zwiazek Kajokowy
Ul. Sienkiewicza 12, (pok.433),
00-101 Warszawa, Poland.
Telephone: 010-48-22-27-49-16
Telex: 813522 Pkol pl (Canoe)

POLYNESIA
International Polynesia Canoe
Federation
PO Box 123, Papeete, Tahiti,
French Polynesia.

PORTUGAL
Federacao Portuguesa de
Canoagem,
Rua Antonio Pinto Machado 60,
4100 Porto, Portugal.

RUMANIA
Federatia Romana de Caiac-
Canoe
Str. Vasile Conta 16, 70139
Bucarest, Rumania.
Telephone: 010-40-0-11-79-70
Telex: 11180 Sport R (Canoe)

SENEGAL
Federation Senegalaise de
Regates
DP 517 Dakar, Senegal.

SINGAPORE
Singapore Canoe Association
585, North Bridge Road, 10-03
Blanco Court,
Singapore 0718.
Telex: 23947 RS

SOVIET UNION
Canoe Federation of the USSR
Loujnetzkaya Nab 8, Moscow,
USSR.
Telephone: 0107-095-201-19-72
Telex: 411287 Konki su (Canoe)

SPAIN
Federacion Espagnola de
Piraguismo
Cea Bermudez 14, lo,28003,
Madrid 3, Spain.
Telephone: 010-34-1-25-30-602
(3,4)
Telex: 2261 Sport Es

SWEDEN
Svenska Kanotforrbundet
Idrotens Hus, 123 87 Farsta,
Sweden.
Telephone: 010-46-8-713-63-55
Telex: 12043 Sports S (Canoe)

SWITZERLAND
Schweizerischer Kanu-Verband
Obere Rebgasse 570, CH-4314,
Zeiningen, Switzerland.
Telephone: 010-41-61-88-20-00

UNITED STATES OF AMERICA
7217 Lockport Place, P.O.B. 248,
Lorton,
Virginia 22079, USA.
Telephone:
0101-684-703-550-7523

URUGUAY
Federacion Uruguaya de Canotaje
Canelones 978, Casa de los
Deportes,
Montevideo, Uruguay.
Telephone: 010-598-90 82 55 (Int.
23)
Telex: (32) 982 COURU UY
(CANOE)

VENEZUELA
Federation Venzolana de Canotaje
y Remo
Apartado de Coreos Nr 75224,
Caracas 10701, Venezuela.

YUGOSLAVIA
Kajakaski Savez Jugoslavije
Bulevar Revolucije 44,
11000 Beograd, Yugoslavia.
Telephone: 010-38-11-553-173
Telex: 11984 Olymp Yu (Canoe)

GLOSSARY

aerated water river water filled with rising air bubbles caused by turbulence.

aerobic exercise muscular activity which is fuelled by oxygen.

anaerobic exercise muscular activity occurring at such an intense rate that fuel is delivered without the utilization of oxygen. It can be maintained for only a short period of time, and oxygen is eventually required for recovery at the end of the period of exercise.

anterior the front aspect of the body.

anti-implosion bar a stiffener across the skirt of a spray cover to prevent it from collapsing under the pressure of water.

asymmetric blades kayak paddles with blades shaped so that right and left cannot be interchanged.

back tow the area of water on the downstream side of a stopper which is flowing upstream.

balance (boat balance) the tilt or lack of tilt of the kayak from sitting level on the water.

bank support (team) land-based assistants acting as rescue cover and support on a white-water venture.

bivouac bag a waterproof and windproof fabric bag which can enclose a person or two for basic shelter. Frequently carried for emergencies.

blind seam waterproof seam in neoprene products such as wetsuits or spray decks.

boils surges of vertically rising water which give confused and unpredictable currents on the surface. Common near deep stoppers and on eddy lines in high-volume rivers.

brace the use of the paddle blade held horizontally on the surface to give support or recovery from instability.

breaking-in entering the current from an eddy so as to carry on downstream.

breaking-out pulling the kayak out of the current into an eddy.

broadsiding running sideways on to an obstruction in the current, such as a boulder.

'cag' paddling jacket worn under the bouyancy aid as a windproof and water-resistant barrier.

canoe polo a ball game for two teams of five aside. The players use short kayaks and score by throwing the ball against a suspended board. It is most commonly played in indoor swimming pools.

carbon fibre 'hi-tech' reinforcement material used to strengthen kayaks and to construct paddle shafts and blades.

carving the path of a kayak turn when it corresponds to the gentle curve of the keel line.

checking stroke a single forward power stroke used at the end of a break-out sequence to counter rearward drift on the boat.

chest harness a quick-release rig worn over, or integrated into, the buoyancy aid to provide a safe method of attachment of the paddler to a rope either for his/her rescue or to help a fellow paddler.

chin cup a plastic moulding threaded on to the chinstrap of a helmet.

circuit training a form of general land conditioning using up to fifteen different exercises in a circuit. Exercises of low-skill intensity are used and the performers are usually timed for a fixed number of circuits.

closed-cell foam non-absorbent foam material used in its flexible form to provide the flotation in buoyancy aids or in stiffer blocks to give rigidity and flotation to kayaks.

coach a kayaking coach is a person who has the experience and knowledge to improve paddlers' individual performances in addition merely to teaching or instructing new techniques.

composite blade a type of paddle blade construction which uses a combination of materials such as aluminium alloy, expanded plastic, and fibreglass to give an extremely strong white-water paddle.

compound stroke a stroke which combines a number of boat-controlling possibilities in sequence.

CPR (cardio-pulmonary resuscitation) mouth-to-mouth resuscitation combined with chest compression to assist the heart.

cross a fast, cross-current move in the kayak. In effect, a high-speed ferry glide.

cushion wave curling wave on the upstream side of a boulder.

drag line a rescue line spanning the river and held on both banks to position a rope accurately. The line is sometimes weighted to take it on to the river bed or clipped to a bouyancy aid to give the line extra flotation and visibility.

dry drowning a term sometimes used to describe drowning when a laryngo-spasm has occurred.

dry suit paddling suit which is worn over a layer of insulating clothing keeping it dry and therefore avoiding loss of insulation. Cold-weather alternative to a wetsuit.

dumbell a short bar used in weight training for one-handed exercises.

eddy any area of slack or counter-moving water in the presence of the main flow.

eddy line the zone of water which separates the slack eddy water from the main flow of the river.

eddy line spin a 360 degree turn on the kayak by lying it across the eddy line. Usually used as an exercise to develop boat accuracy and balance.

eddy line target an imaginary point on the eddy line at which the paddler aims to cross to make a break-out.

edging tilting the kayak using the hips and thighs.

ender and backender standing the kayak vertically using the sloping face of a wave or the downward suction of a stopper.

entrapment a rescue situation where a kayak has stuck vertically or horizontally resulting in trapping the paddler inside either due to water pressure or deformity of the kayak.

epoxy adhesive an extremely strong multipurpose glue which can be used for many different types of repair work in kayaking.

ferry glide crossing the current so as not to lose ground downstream.

forward power stroke a stroke which drives the kayak forward and has the minimum of turning effect.

freestyle kayaking tricks, agilities, and manoeuvres performed in the kayak for fun, light relief, and sometimes serious training.

glass fibre a term used rather loosely to describe the method of boat construction where woven reinforcement, such as glass fibre, is impregnated with resin and hardened inside a mould

green wave a hump of solid, non-aerated water. A standing wave.

haystack a standing wave with a cascading peak.

hip movement the term used to describe rotation of the pelvis which causes the kayak to return to the upright after a roll or brace.

hole a stopper created on the downstream side of a boulder.

hull the underside of the kayak.

hypothermia lowering of the body core temperature as a result of immersion, exhaustion, or both.

ICF International Canoe Federation, the governing body for canoeing and kayaking worldwide. It is concerned mostly with competition.

isokinetic machine Strength- and fitness-conditioning machine. The paddler operates pulley handles which have finely adjustable resistances. The pulling and pushing movements of kayaking can be reproduced accurately on this equipment.

jet another term used to describe a tongue of fast water usually between two eddies.

karabiner a metal link developed for mountaineering to make quick connections with ropes and tapes.

kayak the most commonly

accepted definition of kayak is: a decked boat which is propelled by double-bladed paddles.

kayak volume (high, low, medium) the amount of air, in litres, which is enclosed by the empty kayak shell.

keyhole cockpit a kayak cockpit built for ease of exit of the paddler. Sometimes referred to as a safety cockpit.

laryngo-spasm an instinctive survival reflex which sometimes occurs in the larynx when water is suddenly taken into the mouth. It shuts off the windpipe and prevents anything (including air) from entering the lungs.

latex natural rubber from which the neck, wrist, and ankle seals are made in a drysuit.

loop an ender where the kayak continues beyond the vertical into a somersault.

lead-in the area of water and the sequence of moves which determine the entrance to a rapid.

leaning shifting the bodyweight laterally from the upright, usually to counteract the forces in a tight turn.

multigym a weight-training machine which uses levers with different movements to supply the resistance, rather than free-standing bars and discs.

neoprene a synthetic rubber containing air bubbles. It comes in sheets of varying thicknesses and is used to make wetsuits and spray decks.

nose cone protective shield fitted to the nose of the kayak.

on-sight paddling running a stretch of unfamiliar river by reading the water and making route choices from the kayak rather than by inspecting from the bank first.

oxygen deficit or debt the period of recovery following a burst of anaerobic exercise such as flat-out paddling.

pivot turn A fast turn created by standing the kayak on end and rotating it in this vertical position.

plunge pool the piece of water which becomes the landing area

for a kayak coming over a drop.

polyester a plastic used extensively in the manufacture of outdoor clothing. Polyester fibres form the synthetic fur used in the extremely hard-wearing insulating fabric known a fibrepile. Synthetic fleece is similarly made.

polythene plastic material from which most modern white-water kayaks are constructed.

polypropylene another member of the plastic family. Commonly used in helmet construction but also used to make excellent non-absorbent underwear.

pop-out another name for a skyrocket.

ramp any sloping platform of water might be referred to as a ramp.

rocker the curve along the keel line of a kayak.

rooster tail A curved fountain of water pointing downstream with a pocket of air underneath, indicating an obstruction below the surface such as a rock, log, or even a paddler.

S-cross a cross on a jet combining the break-in followed by break-out manoeuvre of the S-turn with the speed of a simple cross. The paddler usually makes use of a standing wave to lift the kayak at the mid-point in the cross.

seal launch launching off the bank after first getting into the kayak and fixing the spray deck.

sideslip the sideways movement of a kayak across the water.

side surfing riding sideways-on to the current in the slot of a stopper.

skyrocket the pop-out, vertical movement of the kayak which occurs as a reaction to the rear end being sucked downwards in a stopper slot.

sling continuous tape loop used for making quick attachments to anchorages.

slot the deep groove of a stopper and the point at which the downstream flow meets the upstream-moving back-tow.

sluice a term sometimes used to describe an artificial vertical drop in the river which has high sides forming a narrow channel.

snow melt the natural run-off of thawed snow which fills many white-water rivers in spring and summer. Glacial snow melt feeds a river every day throughout the summer so long as there is sunshine.

split paddles kayak paddle which can be separated at a joint in the middle of the shaft to make it easy to carry. Normally stored inside the kayak for emergencies.

spooning shaping of paddle blade to give better purchase on the forward stroke.

spray deck skirt the section of the spray deck which closes off the cockpit space.

squirt boat a kayak of extremely low volume designed to submerge easily at either end so as to make it very willing to stand on its nose or tail.

stopper a vertically circulating eddy of water which shows an area of upstream-returning water on the surface.

strainer a mesh of submerged tree branches with the current flowing through it. A definite hazard to swimmers.

S-turn moving from one eddy to another across a tongue of water by using a break-in followed by a break-out.

tongue a stream of fast water between two eddies.

tow-back or back-tow the section of upstream-returning water which is visible on the surface.

trim the level in the boat's keel. Carrying equipment or forward and rearward body-lean alter the kayak's trim.

vacuum moulding a less common construction process for polyethylene kayaks where the semimoulten plastic inside the mould is blown into position rather than thrown by a rotating mould.

velcro a two-part fastening tape used for closures on clothing.

waterfall jumping kayaking sections of rivers which contain waterfalls.

wave a hump in the flowing water caused by the energy of the river as it accelerates or changes direction.

weir (low-head dam) an artificial ledge on the river creating a sudden fall in the river. Those with vertical faces can be very hazardous in high-water conditions.

FURTHER READING

Technical: boat handling and reading white water
Mason, Bill. 1986. *The Path of the Paddle*. Key Porter Books, Toronto.
Nealy, W. 1986. *Kayak*. Menasha Ridge Press.
Watters, R. 1984. *The White Water River Book*. Pacific Search Press, Seattle.

Competition
British Canoe Union Slalom Committee. *Slalom Canoeing: an introduction*. BCU Supplies, Flexel House, Addlestone, Surrey.
Endicott, B. 1980. *To Win the Worlds*. Reese Press, Baltimore.

Safety and rescue
Alpine Kayak Club. 1983. *Kanu-Gefahren* (written in German). Munich.
American Canoe Association. *The River Safety Task Force Newsletter*. ACA Inc., PO Box 248, Lorton, Virginia.
Bechdel and Ray. 1985. *River Rescue*. Appalachian Mountain Club, Boston.
Rowe, R. 1986. *The Throwline and its Uses in White Water Canoeing*. BCU Supplies, Addlestone, Surrey.

Expeditioning
Deschner, W. 1981. *Does the Wet Suit You?* Eddie Tern Press, Seattle.
Jacobson, W. *Canoeing Wild Rivers*. ICS Books Inc., Indiana.

Guidebooks
Bradt and Jordan. *South America River Trip*. 1 and 2.
Ford, T. 1985. *Austria and Bavaria White Water Guide. Canoeist* magazine.
Lochead and Todd. 1986. *Scottish White Water. Canoeist* magazine.
Pratt-Johnson. 1984. *White Water Trips, Vancouver Island*.
Pratt-Johnson. 1987. *White Water Trips, British Columbia*.
Storry, T. 1987. *Snowdonia, White Water, Sea and Surf*. Cicerone Press.

Training and conditioning
Anderson, B. 1981. *Stretching*. Pelham Books, London. Shelter Publications.
NCF. 1986. *Physiology and Performance. Coaching Handbook*. National Coaching Foundation, Leeds.

INDEX

Numbers in *italics* refer to illustrations

A

abseil launch *80*
accidents 96-105
  see also rescues *and* safety
    aerobic exercise 87, 90
Afon Pen-Llafar (Wales) *43*
air transportation 17
airbags *10, 12,* 13, *103*
anaerobic exercise 87, 90
angle of approach 58, *59*
anti-implosion bar *20,* 21
Arkansas, River (USA) *70*
arm extension *44,* 45, *45*

B

back supports *10,* 11-12
back tow *101,* 102, *102*
backenders 71
balance 58, 60
bank scouring *40*
bank support *108, 109*
bar footrest 13, *13*
bench press 92, *92*
bends 40, *40,* 67-8, *67*
Bio Bio, River (Chile) *40*
bivouac bag *94,* 95
body temperature 21-3, 110-11
body-tow systems 107
body weight and build 10
exercises *see* weight training
boils 33
boulders *see* rocks
bow pull *48,* 49
bow rudder 45, 48-9, *48, 49,* 56, 57, *57, 59*
brace positions 51-2, *51, 52,* 58-9, *67*
break-away cockpit *103*
breaking in 56, *56, 57, 58*
  reverse 59, *59*
breaking out 56-7, *57, 58*
  reverse 59-60, *59*
breathing 102, 110-11
bridges 41
broadsiding *66,* 67, *67, 68*
bulkhead footrest 14
buoyancy aids 18-19, *18,* 100-101, *106*

C

'cag' *21,* 22
canoe tape 27

capsizes 51, 53-5, *54-5,* 65-6, *65,* 100
carbon fibre paddles *25,* 26
cardio-pulmonary resuscitation 110-11
carrying equipment in kayaks *12,* 26-7, *27, 99*
carrying kayaks 14-17, *14-15, 16-17*
carving *47,* 48
Chattooga, River (USA) *74-5*
checking strokes 49
chest harness 106-107, *106*
choice of kayak 10, *10*
circuit training 90
circulation 109-11
Cirotteau, François 76
clothing 21-4, *21-4*
  for eskimo roll 54
  spare 95
cockpit 11-13, *12,* 21
cold 110-11
  see also hypothermia
communication between paddlers 108
competitive kayaking 112-16, *112-13*
  safety 18, 116
compound strokes 40
construction of kayaks 10
control 44-55, 82
Conway Gorge (Wales) *76*
co-ordination 45
cotton clothing 23
cross, the 61, *61*
  on a wave 62, *62*
crossing current 60-2, *61*
crossing uneven current 60-1
curl exercise 91, *91*
current
  crossing 60-2, *61*
  entering *see* breaking in
  exiting *see* breaking out
  helical 41
cushion wave 34, *35,* 40, *40, 66,* 67, *67*

D

deck lines 14
deep circulation *36*
Deschener, Whit 70
design of kayaks 8, 10
diolene *9*
Dixon, Sue 76
down pulls 92, *93*
downstream 'V' shape 34, *34, 37*
draw stroke 50-1, *50,* 51
drops *78*
  equipment for 81-2, *80, 81*
  large 77-9, *79*
  small 72-7, *74, 77*
drowning 109-11

drysuit 22-3, *23*
dumb bell 92, *92*
Durance, River (France) *39*

E

eddy 28, *29,* 33, *33, 39,* 56-61, *57, 58, 59*
  hopping 86
  vertical 34
eddy line 28, *29,* 33, 56, 57-9, *57, 58, 59*
  draw 86
  spin 60, *60*
  target 57-8, *58*
eddy turns 48, *48,* 49, 56, 58-9
edging *46,* 48, 49
elbow pads 82
elbow turn 82, *82*
end paddler 108
enders 71, *71,* 84, *84,* 86
endurance training 87, 90
entrapment 102-105, *103, 104, 105,* 107
equipment
  carrying 26-7, *27, 99*
  checks 44
  drops 81-2, *80, 81*
  rescue 94-5, 106-108, *106, 107*
  for rolls 54
  safety 94-5, *94*
  for wild-water racing 113-14
eskimo roll 53-5, *54,* 65-6

F

fear 82
'feel' 84
ferry glide 60, *60,* 61, *61*
  reverse 61
fibreglass kayaks *9,* 10, 14, *27, 103*
fibreglass paddles *25,* 26
first-aid kit *94,* 95, 105, *110*
fitness training 84, 87-93
flat-topped wave 32, *32*
flexibility 87
floating a boat on a line *100*
flotation *12,* 13
  personal *see* buoyancy aids
footrests *10,* 13-14, *13,* 81, *81*
footwear 24, *24*
forward paddling 44-5, *44, 45, 46*
forward sweep stroke 45-6, *46*
Fox, Alan *72*
freestyling 71, 84, *84,* 86
  tricks 84, 86

G

General, River (Costa Rica) *31*
grab handles *11,* 14

Photographic Acknowledgements

Alan Fox Collection: title page; Peter Greenland Photography: 9, 12, 18, 19, 21, 22, 23, 24, 25, 26, 33 (bottom), 45, 46, 47, 48, 48-9, 51, 52, 52-3 (top), 56, 57, 58, 59, 61, 62, 63 (bottom), 66, 67, 68, 71, 73, 76, 78, 90, 91, 92, 96 (top), 97 (top left, top right, centre), 98, 98-9, 99, 104 (right), 105, 106; Slim Ray: 6, 30-1 (top), 40-1, 74-5; Ray Rowe: 15, 16, 28, 29, 30 (bottom), 31 (bottom), 32 (bottom), 32-3 (top), 34-5, 36 (bottom), 36-7 (top), 37 (top and bottom), 38, 38-9 (bottom), 39, 40, 42-3, 43, 63 (top), 64, 69, 70, 72-3, 76 (top), 79, 80, 81, 83, 84, 85, 86, 95, 96 (bottom), 97 (bottom), 100-1, 101, 103, 104, (left), 109, 110; Tony Tickle: 112, 113, 116, 116-7, 117.

PRINTED IN BELGIUM BY
proost
INTERNATIONAL BOOK PRODUCTION